Jim Reeve is a friend, but to a wnly me. He is becoming a trusted [...] ing number of people as his cong[...] [...]he visionary leadership, hope-build...ing ...cacting and Bible-based solidity his ministry is providing a new generation.

This book is a sampling of something good for your soul—something I guarantee will be more enduring, and probably even more enjoyable, than today's various mixes of "chicken soup" spirituality. That's not a criticism—just a fact—so read and be filled.

—JACK W. HAYFORD, CHANCELLOR
THE KING'S COLLEGE AND SEMINARY

This book is an exciting and much needed scriptural explanation to the age-old question, "Is God there when we hurt?" Pastor Jim Reeve eloquently and clearly provides both scriptural and practical answers in a quick-reading and uplifting manner. This book is one that, even once you have read it, you will want to keep close by to refer to during the trials and tribulations that occur in everyone's life. I have often said that what I thought were the valleys were actually the mountains, and this great book paints that picture masterfully.

—TOMMY BARNETT, SENIOR PASTOR
PHOENIX FIRST ASSEMBLY OF GOD

This book offers the healing comfort of God for your deepest hurts. It shows how God can bring good results out of your worst situations if you will trust Him.

—RICK WARREN, SENIOR PASTOR
SADDLEBACK CHURCH

Let's be honest—everybody has bumps, scrapes and bruises. Jim Reeve demonstrates how God not only brings comfort, but also turns what could be our tombstones into stepping-stones. *God Never Wastes a Hurt* will encourage you to become the champion God intends you to be!

—JOHN MAXWELL
AUTHOR

GOD NEVER
WASTES A HURT

-JIM REEVE-

GOD NEVER WASTES A HURT by Jim Reeve
Published by Creation House
A part of Strang Communications Company
600 Rinehart Road
Lake Mary, Florida 32746
www.creationhouse.com

Unless otherwise noted, all Scripture quotations are from the Holy Bible, New International Version. Copyright © 1973, 1978, 1984, International Bible Society. Used by permission.

Scripture quotations marked KJV are from the King James Version of the Bible.

Scripture quotations marked NKJV are from the New King James Version of the Bible. Copyright © 1979, 1980, 1982 by Thomas Nelson, Inc., publishers. Used by permission.

Library of Congress Catalog Card Number: 00-109168
International Standard Book Number: 0-88419-738-7

Incidents and persons portrayed in this book are based on fact. Some names, places and any identifying details may have been changed and altered to protect the privacy and anonymity of the individuals to whom they refer. Any similarity between the names and stories of individuals known to readers is coincidental and not intentioned.

0 1 2 3 4 5 6 7 VERSA 8 7 6 5 4 3 2 1
Printed in the United States of America

❧

To my wife, Marguerite, God's gift of love and strength to me

To my children, Dan, Julie and Jeff,
and my daughter-in-law, Amy,
who bring joy for today and hope for tomorrow

To my grandson, Eyan, who is way too much fun

To the people of Faith Community Church,
living testimonies that *God Never Wastes a Hurt*

To my mom, Patricia Reeve, who never ceases
to amaze me with her faith and courage

And to my father, Charles Reeve,
who modeled for me how to be a husband,
father, pastor and man of God. Thanks, Dad!

Contents

❧

Section I
Tribs Happen

Chapter 1

God of the Valleys

"Call an ambulance!" one of the ushers yelled from the aisle. Somebody else was laying Dad down on the floor and starting CPR. It all seemed like a dream—no, more like a nightmare.

Only seconds earlier my wife Marguerite and I were walking up on stage to do announcements for Faith Community's Twenty-Year Anniversary Celebration Service. It was an especially happy day, and the platform looked beautiful covered with decorations and balloons. Dad and Mom had helped me start the church back in 1980. For the past twenty years they had been instrumental in helping thousands of people's hurts to be healed and dreams restored.

Dad had just finished baptizing two people and had stood in the front row, joining in the worship that had been particularly good for this special celebration. As everyone was being seated, those around my dad motioned for my attention. As I looked at him, I could immediately tell something was wrong—seriously wrong.

"I'm sorry for stopping the service, but something is the

1

matter with my dad," I somehow managed to announce to the congregation. "Please get in groups and pray for him while we wait for the paramedics."

It was six long minutes before the ambulance arrived. The worship team on stage played softly as hundreds of people interceded for Dad—Pastor Chuck. Despite the best efforts of the paramedics and hospital emergency staff, despite our fervent prayers and immediate CPR—Dad died. The doctors used the term cardiac arrest. All I knew is that one minute he was worshiping the Lord—and the next minute he was in the presence of the Lord.

It still does not make any sense, Dad's dying right in the middle of our church service—right in front of my eyes. Dad was in perfect health—the youngest sixty-eight-year-old that you have ever seen. His dad, my grandpa, is doing great at ninety-four years of age. And my grandpa's father lived to be ninety-two. Mom and Dad's fiftieth wedding anniversary was only months away. Their first great-grandson, Eyan, had just been born two days earlier. Dad had everything to live for.

For over twenty years thousands have shared with me how they have gained victory as they walked through some of the darkest valleys imaginable because of the truths I have taught them. Teaching about how God never wastes a hurt is a whole lot easier than living it. The principles I have faithfully taught others—and have learned to walk in myself—are not just nice ideas; they are indispensable truths that deliver us from death to life.

VALLEYS: A GOOD GOD CAN BRING GOOD THINGS OUT OF BAD TIMES

Every person walks through valleys, those places of diffi-culty and suffering where we feel lonely, God-forsaken and hurt. In the valleys, fear and doubt become our traveling companions. Some valleys are deeper and longer than others, perhaps caused by the death of a child or a loved one. Others are shorter and more manageable, more of a hassle than a genuine hardship. Some bring on a mild case of the blues; others are so painful that we yearn to die.

Life has a way of beating us up—no matter how much faith we have, no matter what spiritual camp we are in, no matter how many demons we cast out or how many "words from the Lord" we receive. Even for the believer, then, life is a mixture of pain and pleasure, victory and defeat, success and failure, mountain peaks and valleys. We are not bad people merely because we are experiencing stress and frustration. We are simply people. Welcome to the human race!

Every one of us has hidden hurts that no one else knows about. A woman told me once, "When I walked up the aisle to marry the man of my dreams and start a new life, I didn't realize how much emotional baggage was underneath my beautiful makeup and white dress." Because we carry these wounds with us wherever we go, neither new surroundings nor new relationships bring the relief we so long for. Neither a brave smile nor a stiff upper lip can remove the reality that all of us have bumps, scrapes and bruises. And the sooner we become honest about this, the sooner we can discover our way out.

Valleys are nothing new, nor are the particular problems we face today all that different from the problems of yesterday. The Bible alludes to several of life's valleys that are as real today as they were thousands of years ago, including:

- The Valley of Calamity (Josh. 7:26)
- The Valley of Giants (Josh. 15:8)
- The Valley of Weeping (Ps. 84:6)
- The Valley of Dry Bones (Ezek. 37:1)
- The Valley of the Shadow of Death (Ps. 23)

Of all the valleys in the Bible, probably the most well-known is the one found in Psalm 23. Because at one time or another all of us must face our own mortality, the beautifully poetic words of this passage touch saint and sinner alike. I have been in hospitals chatting with unabashed non-Christians who were lying on their deathbeds, and they have surprised me by reciting from memory this psalm. Maybe it is only a vague recollection from their childhood or a lasting remnant of something their mother taught them. From whatever source, in response to my asking them if they know anything about the Bible, they quietly start quoting: "The LORD is my shepherd; I shall not want…Yea, though I walk through the valley of the shadow of death, I will fear no evil: for thou art with me" (Ps. 23:1, 4, KJV).

I suspect nonbelievers somehow have a sense, perhaps a persistent hope, that help is available even while facing the deepest and darkest of valleys. It is told how W. C. Fields, the famous comedian of early cinema and an avowed atheist, was "caught" reading the Bible on his deathbed. With his stereotyped comedic voice he said, "Looking for loopholes."

David wrote the Twenty-third Psalm from personal experience. Sheep were safe with David, no matter where their journeys took them. He cared for his flock, keeping them healthy and well fed. If necessary, he protected them. David had risked his own life for his flock, killing a lion and bear on two separate occasions using only his bare hands. David had been a good shepherd to his sheep, but more importantly, he knew that he too had a Good Shepherd watching over him, no matter where his journeys took him

David had an unrelenting belief that God was good. This conviction sustained him during those times when life seemed anything but good. There is an old Arab proverb that says, "All sunshine and no rain make a desert." This is not simply a case of "when life gives you lemons, make lemonade," but rather a sense that just maybe a good God can bring good things out of bad times. David knew that valleys were not just something to *go* through, but to *grow* through.

I have traveled to Israel and visited a valley called the Valley of the Shadow of Death. Whether or not this is the valley that David was referring to, we don't know, but the canyon is so narrow and deep that the sun shines on the floor for only moments a day. The rest of the time the canyon is covered in shadows, sometimes very dark shadows.

Many of us are in valleys like that. A valley to David would be like a dark alley to us. All the fear and danger associated with an alley—that's what David meant. We have all seen TV shows where a woman gets off work late in a bad part of town and decides to take a shortcut to her car through an alleyway. Invariably, something bad happens, and she has to run from some sort of lowlife she bumped into there.

God says that even if we find ourselves in one of those situations, we do not have to fear evil.

Are you going through a tough time? Do you feel as if your life is falling apart? That is a valley, and life is full of them. Don't despair! Millions have been through them, and you too will emerge better, stronger and healthier than you went in. God will not waste that valley, but He will raise you up to a high place to teach others what you have learned.

GOD SAYS WE ARE
HYPER-CONQUERORS: IN THE FINAL ANALYSIS WE WIN

There is no map that gives us directions around all the valleys—that's the bad news. The good news is that while we go through valleys, God will be with us, and through faith we can come out the other side victorious. Romans 8:37 promises believers that life's problems can never, in the end, win: "No, in all these things we are more than conquerors through him who loved us." The phrase "more than conquerors" is only one word in the Greek. This one word is so intensive that it takes several English words to translate it. It begins with the prefix *huper,* from which we get the English prefix *hyper.* It means "more," or "to the point of excess." If we have particularly active children who are a challenge to parent, we say those children are "hyperactive," or just plain "hyper." Some people have a thyroid that may cause them trouble if it becomes hyperactive. Commercials tell us that we at times do not suffer from mere tension, but hypertension.

In the same way, the Bible says that in God we are not simply winners and conquerors, but hyper-conquerors. Think about it—God does not declare His children to be victors on occasion or by the slimmest of margins, but rather champions who relentlessly defeat their opponents. That does not mean there will not be valleys, and it does not mean we will not face difficulties along the way. It simply means that in the final analysis the valleys do not win—we do!

DON'T DOUBT IN THE DARK
WHAT GOD HAS TOLD YOU IN THE LIGHT

At one point I was going through a particularly discouraging period in my life and ministry. I was overwhelmed, and I felt like giving up, quitting and running away to "lick my wounds" and pout. My wife, Marguerite, reminded me that God had spoken clearly to us about starting Faith Community Church. "We need to go back to the last point we heard God speak to us," Marguerite encouraged me. "God plainly spoke to us about starting Faith Community. He hasn't said one word to us about giving up." She was right. Never doubt in the dark what God has told you in the light.

God of the Valleys

Have you ever had a mountaintop experience with God that left you feeling high? You may have attended a conference or a meeting and had a significant moment with the Almighty. God's Word to you was powerful, and your course seemed clear. Still, two weeks later you thought, *Here I am, back like I was before! God's presence and will for my life are as vague as ever. What happened to the clear view I had on the summit?* Reality reminds us that between every mountaintop experience is a valley through which God takes us. The key is to not forget what God said and did during that mountaintop experience.

Be honest with yourself: Mountaintop experiences are the hot fudge sundaes of life, but faith grows and is strengthened in the valleys. Valleys are the green beans and asparagus, the elements that make us grow. I have to admit in hindsight I am thankful for the valleys I have gone through because they have made me a better man. No, they were not fun to go through at the time, and I am certain that, if given the choice now, I would probably choose to avoid future valleys.

But we do not have that choice, and if we are to live well, we need to get a handle on what these valleys are, what they mean and how to get through them. We need to understand that our experiences are never wasted, even the difficult and painful ones, if we allow God to use them.

There are five things about valleys I want us to consider.

1. Valleys are not optional—"Tribs happen."

American consumers are spoiled. We take for granted multiple options. We get to choose not only what we want, but also the type, color and flavor. All of life, so we think, should come in thirty-one flavors! But we soon discover that life does not come to us as easily or conveniently as our fast food or brand-name clothes.

There is not a person on this planet who skates through

life problem-free. And Christians are subject to the same terms and conditions as everyone else.

If you are like me, when you get hit with something, your first response is to wonder, "What did I do wrong?" Even though I know in my head that life dishes it out to everyone, I still get angry and say, "Come on, God! I'm trying to get stuff done here. Why did You hit me with this? And why now? Why don't You pick someone else? Did I do something bad to deserve this?" In short, we all are tempted to think, *This is not what I ordered!*

The blame game is easy, isn't it? If life is not delivering what we expect, we tend to think someone somewhere messed up. Some constantly blame themselves, convincing themselves that if they were simply better people, life would not treat them so harshly. Others are convinced someone else is to blame. No matter how bad we are, we can always think of someone worse and wish our troubles on them!

Jesus said in John 16:33, "In the world you will have tribulation" (NKJV). I like to call that the "tribs." Jesus promised us "tribs." Now there's a verse we do not have to name and claim to make it operate in our lives. We do not have to walk around saying, "I'm claiming John 16:33 and believing God for the tribs." To misquote Forrest Gump and that famous bumper sticker, "Tribs happen!"

Tribs are not optional; they are part of the curriculum of life. Valleys are not "electives," nor are they necessarily punishment for something we or someone else has done wrong. They are essential elements for our growth. God knows we cannot get from where we are to where He wants to take us without them. In fact, those personally trained by Jesus learned that tribs are actually a good and welcome thing. James noted, "Consider it pure joy, my brothers, whenever you face trials of many kinds" (James 1:2). Peter said, "Dear friends, do not be surprised at the painful trial you are suffering, as though something strange were happening to you" (1 Pet. 4:12).

In other words, because valleys are not optional, do not be shocked when you find yourself in the middle of a situation in which there seems to be no way out. Rather than whining, complaining and wondering, *Why me?,* with joy look to what God is producing in you. No matter what your biggest challenge is—money, marriage, family or health—you are not the first person ever to face that dilemma, and your problem is not the worst in the history of humankind. Remember when facing valleys that you were forewarned. Jesus did promise that in the world you would have tribulation, but He quickly added the command to "cheer up." Why? Because He promised us that He had overcome the world.

Some Christians mistakenly believe that tribs should not come in a believer's life—if that believer has "faith." When something terrible happens, or when they go through a hard time emotionally, some Spirit-filled Christians pretend it isn't happening. Others deny the problem is real; they hope that the problem will go away and that the valley will end simply by ignoring it. They may wear a smile at church and claim the promises at work, but all too often they weep on their pillows at night.

At some point, someone has to have the courage to acknowledge the biblical truth that tribs happen to everyone—even people of great faith. We all go through valleys and times of legitimate hurt. But if we keep the hope of Christ in our heart, the trial will turn into a triumph.

2. Valleys are not predictable—"Stress and suffering can't be scheduled."

Contrary to what we would like, we cannot schedule the rough times. It would be nice to pencil in times of being blue, times of a death in the family or times of health problems—but life does not offer such a convenience. There is no ATM for stress or suffering, where we can make transactions at our own whim. You cannot schedule heartache as you can an eye appointment. There are no drive-through valleys.

Valleys typically begin unpredictably. Every one of us is one phone call away from our life being turned upside down. We are one doctor's report away from dramatic life changes. We need to put proper perspective on our ability—or more properly our inability—to control our own lives. Jesus said:

> Therefore I tell you, do not worry about your life, what you will eat or drink; or about your body, what you will wear. Is not life more important than food, and the body more important than clothes? Look at the birds of the air; they do not sow or reap or store away in barns, and yet your heavenly Father feeds them. Are you not much more valuable than they? Who of you by worrying can add a single hour to his life?
>
> And why do you worry about clothes? See how the lilies of the field grow. They do not labor or spin. Yet I tell you that not even Solomon in all his splendor was dressed like one of these. If that is how God clothes the grass of the field, which is here today and tomorrow is thrown into the fire, will he not much more clothe you, O you of little faith? So do not worry, saying, "What shall we eat?" or "What shall we drink?" or "What shall we wear?" For the pagans run after all these things, and your heavenly Father knows that you need them. But seek first his kingdom and his righteousness, and all these things will be given to you as well. Therefore do not worry about tomorrow, for tomorrow will worry about itself. Each day has enough trouble of its own.
>
> —MATTHEW 6:25–34

The only predictable thing I find about valleys is that they usually come at the least desirable times. For me, it is when I am already down, tired, bummed and wanting to quit. When did the devil attack Jesus? The most famous temptations in history came immediately following forty days of fasting by our Lord. I am sure this time brought spiritual strength to our Lord, but the Bible nevertheless notes that He was hungry. I bet! My wife claims I get grouchy if I miss lunch. That temptation to turn the stones into bread was no small thing.

Jesus, like many of us, was "hit when He was down." But the Word inside Him was stronger than the valley outside Him. He pressed through and came out the other side a winner. Tired? Yes. Hungry? Yes. Matthew tells us that when the temptations were over God sent angels to minister to His Son (Matt. 4:11).

God does the same with you and me. When we go through tough times, God sees and cares. He has ways of refreshing us, renewing us and putting us back together. Luke adds that when the devil was finished with all his tempting, he left Jesus "until an opportune time" (Luke 4:13). That is like the devil saying, "You win. I'm out of here," and then turning around and saying, "But I'll be back."

As a kid I loved the television show *Candid Camera*. Allen Funt, the host, would close each show with the phrase, "Sometime, somehow, somewhere . . . when you least expect it . . . someone will come up to you and say, 'Smile! You're on *Candid Camera.*'" Life can be like that. Sometime, somehow, somewhere, when we least expect it, something sneaks up and says, "Smile, you're in a valley!"

Although valleys are not predictable, I have noticed that I often get hit right before or right after times of great spiritual breakthrough. When I get hit with bad news or a personal struggle, I have learned to look up because I know the enemy is trying to rob me of something great that God wants to do. He tries to get every one of us off the mountain path before we reach the peak.

If he cannot do that, he will hit us on the way down and try to rob us of the lasting effects of the mountain peak experience. That is why making it through the valley is so important: It shows that the peak experience has truly changed and deepened us as a person.

3. Valleys are not prejudiced—"Bad things happen to good people."

Los Angeles County, where I live and minister, is one of the most ethnically diverse places in the world. The congregation I pastor reflects this diversity, and I have learned through experience that problems and pain are not prejudiced. They afflict people indiscriminately regardless of race, creed, religion or culture. Whites, Blacks, Asians and Latinos are all alike subject to life's pitfalls. The kinds of valleys may differ from group to group, just as a desert valley is different from a tropical valley, but the reality of valleys is the same for everyone.

The same is true concerning the lifestyles of the rich and famous. Neither money nor fame protects people from hurt. "Down and outers" get more attention, but believe me, the world is also full of "up and outers."

- You cannot avoid valleys if you are rich.
- You cannot avoid valleys if you are poor.
- You cannot avoid valleys if you are famous.
- You cannot avoid valleys if you are unknown.

Being a good person does not automatically keep us from hurts either. Jesus said that God "causes his sun to rise on the evil and the good, and sends rain on the righteous and the unrighteous" (Matt. 5:45). Good people and bad people alike have both good times and bad times. The bottom line is that all of us live in a fallen world full of problems and pain as well as the sustaining grace of our Creator. The Southern California sun warms saint and sinner alike. And no one is insulated from pain, sorrow, stress, frustrations, down times, trials and disturbances. Good things happen to bad people, and bad things happen to good people.

4. Valleys are not permanent—"If you don't quit, you won't fail."

We cannot avoid valleys. That's the bad news. The good news is that all valleys end sooner or later. Robert Schuller says tough times never last, but tough people always do! We will make it out of the valleys as long as we do not quit. And we will come out stronger people than we were when we first entered. The clichés are true: It's always too soon to quit. Failure is never final.

It does not matter how painful, difficult or stressful the valley is—it will end. So if you feel as if you are going through hell, my advice to you is, "Well then, don't stop there." You have heard the saying: "When you're going through hell, don't stop. When you catch hell, don't hold it."

First Peter 1:5 declares that God's children "through faith are shielded by God's power." The very fact we are shielded means we are being hit with stuff. However, no matter what we are hit with or what we have to go through, God promises His protection. This means that although we may experience pain and discomfort, ultimately we are protected. No wonder we can walk through the valley with confidence.

Peter goes on to note that God's protective shield is promised "until the coming of salvation that is ready to be revealed in the last time. In this you greatly rejoice" (vv. 5–6). We rejoice during the tough times, then, for two reasons: One, God is shielding us so that not only can we survive, but we also grow; and two, salvation is on the way. So if you are currently in a valley, take heart. God will protect you until this thing comes to an end—and it will end!

Severity can make valleys seem longer than they really are. Time seems to come almost to a standstill when we are really hurting. Physical and emotional pain turn minutes into hours and hours into days. These are the times when it is most important to remember that even the most severe of valleys is temporary and that God is protecting us all the while.

The apostle Paul knew firsthand not only the highest highs but also the lowest lows that life had to offer. His words, spoken like the words of an experienced warrior, ought to encourage the most fainthearted:

> Therefore we do not lose heart. Though outwardly we are wasting away, yet inwardly we are being renewed day by day. For our light and momentary troubles are achieving for us an eternal glory that far outweighs them all.
> —2 CORINTHIANS 4:16–17

Claudia grew up with a father who did not love her, who would get drunk and frequently violent with her mother. One time, in a fit of guilt, he called Claudia and her sister into the kitchen and announced he was going to kill himself for being such a bad person. He sent them to their rooms where they sat silently listening to their father and mother fight. Suddenly, they heard a gunshot. They thought he had shot their mother, but they were not sure since they could still hear two voices. He had put a bullet through the ceiling, and was later taken to the hospital for overdosing on aspirin.

Over time Claudia tried to earn his love, but nothing worked. She became the perfect student, quiet and attentive in class, thinking that maybe this would bring the attention she so desired. All it really did was hide the pain inside. At a young age she had acquired a knowledge of God and would often comfort herself by pretending she was walking down the street holding Jesus' hand. She pictured Him as the big man who protected her.

One day her aunt invited her to church, and Claudia accepted Jesus as her Savior. Her father mocked her for reading the Bible, but she stayed faithful. She continued in church and grew stronger in the faith.

Her parents eventually divorced, and her father met a woman who spoke to him about the Lord. Her father began to go to church with Claudia and her sister. Finally, he too accepted the Lord.

Claudia never gave up. She went to college and became a children's social worker. She has an incredible love for children, and on weekends she teaches a Sunday school class. She knows she beat the odds; she had all the signs of being another sad statistic—someone who repeats the cycle by marrying an abusive alcoholic. But she didn't. She refused to quit, and God honored her perseverance by setting her free.

Claudia acknowledges that her passion for working with children springs from her personal experiences. She has a vision to open Christian foster homes where rejected and hurt kids learn about the love of God.

If this is the worst time in your life, don't stop. It will end. If you do not quit, you will not fail.

5. Valleys are where we find the fruit—"Those who sow in tears reap in joy."

This is perhaps the best part. Go anywhere in the world, and you will see that farmers overwhelmingly prefer to plant in valleys. I have seen farms on steep hillsides where terraces have been built to make the land useful. But overall, the best farming and best fruit are in the valleys.

The spiritual fruit is in the valleys, too. As I said before, my greatest growth as a person has come in the most difficult times of my life. I know that is true for others as well. The fruit of sorrow grows sweet when a believer endures. The Bible says, "Those who sow in tears shall reap in joy" (Ps. 126:5, NKJV). And joy is one of the richest fruits that grow in the valley.

SHADOWS, NOT DEATH

David faced his valleys without fear because he knew the protection of the Good Shepherd. Not only that, but he had discovered the difference between reality and perception. For example, in Psalm 23 the valley is not called the valley of death, but rather the valley of the *shadow* of death. That's a crucial distinction. Shadows can be intimidating, but they are not real.

Keep this in mind about shadows: Shadows are typically bigger than the reality they represent. We all know what it's like to be taking a walk in the late afternoon when the shadows cast by the trees, buildings and even our own bodies are much longer than the objects themselves. A shadow can easily make something that in reality is not all that large appear massive. Therefore, sometimes what we fear the most is not even real. As President Franklin D. Roosevelt said years ago, "The only thing we have to fear is fear itself."[1]

For many of us, our biggest problem is not the hurtful situation; rather, it is how we see the situation. The Bible calls Satan a deceiver, and sometimes his greatest deception is to make himself appear bigger than he really is. Our problems are magnified as we crouch in fear and inaction. The sad thing is that much of it is smoke and mirrors.

The Bible says, "Magnify the Lord with me, and let us exalt His name together" (Ps. 34:3, NKJV). When we praise God, do we really make God any bigger than He already is? Of course not. God is God whether we praise Him or not. But through praise our perception of God is magnified, and our eyes are opened to see that He really is bigger than our hurts.

Shadows do just the opposite: They cause our fear and doubt to be magnified. No valley is bigger than God, and the sooner we look past the shadows into His face the better.

SHADOWS CANNOT HURT YOU

Shadows are like special effects in a Hollywood movie—they are images without substance. Except for maybe making us jump in our seats in surprise, movie monsters cannot hurt anybody. High-speed car chases, narrow escapes from bad guys and close encounters with creatures from another planet have all failed to harm us. Why? They are not real. The same is true of shadows. Have you ever been run over and injured by a shadow? Would you rather be hit by a truck or the shadow of that truck? No one has ever been bruised, cut or harmed by a shadow.

When I was six years old I went to a drive-in movie with my mom and dad. (Anyone still remember drive-in theaters?) We went to see the Alfred Hitchcock movie *Psycho*. Now I suppose that movie is nothing compared to the scary movies they have out today, but for its time, it was frightening enough, especially for a six-year-old kid. My parents wanted me to sleep in the back seat, but I was curious, so I kept popping my head up to watch. I did not want to be scared, so I would only peek when I thought it was safe. I would judge the scary scenes by the movie's soundtrack. When the music stopped or sounded normal, I figured it was safe to look. This worked fine until the end of the movie.

In their attempts to discover the perpetrator of some gruesome murders, the investigators were creeping up the stairs to the upper floor of a creepy old-looking house, hoping to find the caretaker's mother. As they crept up, the music was tense and taut, and from the back seat I was peeking and ducking, peeking and ducking. With every step up the stairs they took, the tension would rise accordingly. Finally, they made it into the bedroom, door creaking, and all they could see was the hair and back of an elderly women—the mother—sitting in a rocking chair. I only know all this now because I have since seen the entire movie. At the time I was bopping and weaving from the back seat of the car.

The scene climaxes with the scariest part of the movie. The rocking chair is turned around, revealing not a motherly old lady but a fully dressed, rotting corpse. Guess when I popped up to look? You guessed it! Just in time to see the disgusting face of the mother's decaying corpse.

That sight went through me like a knife. Later that night I went to bed and had the worst nightmare of my life. I woke up and actually saw, with my six-year-old eyes, the dead lady rocking in my bedroom. I was not asleep, so it was not a dream. Yet there she was, rocking between my bed and the door. Were my eyes playing tricks on me? Was I still dreaming? My little heart was racing.

I knew I had to get to my parents, but the only way out of my room was directly through her. I remember making the decision to run through her to get to the door, so I closed my eyes and ran as fast as I could. In hindsight, I am glad I didn't hit a wall and do some real damage to myself! As it was, I made it to my parents' bedroom and hopped in bed with Mom and Dad. They told me later that I was shaking from head to foot. But as soon as I hit that bed, I knew I was protected. Rotting corpses could not touch me when I was near my daddy's arms. Demons from hell could not touch me now—I was safe.

To this day, I do not know what I saw. I do know this—the

shadow, the image, had frightened me, but I had found refuge in my father's arms. In the end, my father was more real than the image of death. Isn't that what David wrote about? "Even though I walk through the valley of the shadow of death, I will fear no evil." Why? "For you are with me" (Ps. 23:4). God is our refuge, our hiding place. He is the cleft in the rock; I will find safety and security in the secret place of the Most High. For me, that secret place is just like Mom and Dad's bed after a childhood nightmare.

No shadow can exist without light. Part of the key to making it through the valleys is to get our eyes off the shadows and on the light. Jesus is the light of the world. When you fix your eyes on Him, you will find that He is the author and the finisher of our faith, the beginning and the end, the Alpha and the Omega. Corrie ten Boom used to say, "If you look at the world, you'll be depressed. If you look within, you'll be distressed. But if you look at Christ, you'll be at rest."

GOD OF THE VALLEYS: DON'T MESS WITH FATHER GOD

Ahab and Jezebel were quite a pair. The very name *Jezebel* has become synonymous with both wickedness and ruthlessness. Ahab was one of the weakest and most morally bankrupt kings in the Bible. It is not surprisingly, then, that during their reign the nation of Israel was in a constant state of confusion and despair. Yet one incident during their rule illustrates something wonderful about God and the valleys.

Despite the fact Israel was in a backslidden state, in 1 Kings 20 we find God working miraculously on their behalf. Outnumbered and under threat of annihilation, Israel nevertheless overpowers the horses and chariots of the Syrians, inflicting heavy losses on the enemy. It is a supernatural victory orchestrated not by Ahab, but by a prophet and the young officers of Israel. The victory shocks both the victor and the vanquished. Why would God fight for a people who were so clearly compromising their faith?

The answer has to do not only with the grace of God, who often chooses to reveal Himself despite our condition, but the arrogance of the enemy. It might even be said the enemy ticked God off! Sometimes we get blessed not because of who we are but because of God's anger at the enemy. In this case, the Syrians believed they not only faced a weaker opponent in Israel, but a defective God in Israel as well. The Syrians quickly discovered, however, how wrong they were. An old television commercial used to declare, "Don't mess with Mother Nature." Well, the Syrians discovered you "don't mess with Father God."

The first time Syria attacked, Israel surprised King Ben-Hadad and beat him badly—a major upset. The Syrians, licking their wounds, tried to figure out why they lost. Meanwhile the officials of King Ben-Hadad advised him, "Their gods are gods of the hills. That is why they were too strong for us. But if we fight them on the plains, surely we will be stronger than they" (1 Kings 20:23).

The advisors led the Syrians to believe that Israel's God only worked for them in the hills, but that in the valleys the Syrian gods were more powerful. In the natural, they may have been referring to the tactics of warfare. Syrian chariots were certainly less effective on uneven hills than they would be on the flat plains. And perhaps the ground forces of Israel were more effective concealed amidst the trees and rocks of the hills than exposed in the relative open spaces of the valleys.

On another level, however, something else was being said. Hills symbolize the high points of life—the good times if you will—while valleys represent the low. Is the God of Israel only helpful for the good times of life? When the going gets tough, does God leave? The Syrians thought so, and so does the devil. Satan said to God about Job:

> Have you not put a hedge around him and his household and everything he has? You have blessed the work of his hands, so that his flocks and herds are spread throughout the land. But stretch out your hand and strike everything he has, and he will surely curse you to your face.
>
> —JOB 1:10–11

Satan was arguing that the only reason Job loved God was because he had a charmed life—healthy kids, prosperity and the divine blessing. As long as Job was living the high life, of course he would live righteous and serve God. But put him in a valley—in one of those tough experiences of life—and he would curse God.

As long as God's people are on the mountaintop, prospering and feeling good, they are hard to knock out. But when they get in that valley, going through the tribs, their God is an absentee landlord, and they are fair-weather servants.

The temptation to think like the Syrians and Satan is all too real. It is easy to feel that God has lost touch with us in the valleys—that somehow the signal has been scrambled and our call no longer goes through. We have all known days when encouragement never came, days when we went to bed at night as troubled and disappointed as when we woke up.

But God is not just the God of the hills—He is the God of the valleys, your valleys, my valleys. He is a God of the low place and the high place, the mountaintop experience and the grinding frustration of daily life. He is still God, and He is still there when we go through depression, sickness, divorce and addiction. God does not leave us alone in the valleys.

After losing the first battle, the Syrians decide to attack Israel again—this time in the valley. The Syrian king's advisors promised, "Then surely we will be stronger than they" (1 Kings 20:25). It is one thing to get hit when we are strong and feeling good. It is altogether another thing to get punched when we are down and vulnerable. Like the Israelites, we can almost hear our enemies saying, "This time you're going down."

God, however, has a word for our attackers and for us. The Bible says a "man of God" came up to King Ahab and prophesied:

> This is what the LORD says: "Because the Arameans [Syrians] think the LORD is a god of the hills and not a God of the valleys, I will deliver this vast army into your hands, and you will know that I am the LORD."
>
> —1 KINGS 20:28

I want to be a "man of God" for you and your situation right now and declare the same promise to you. God is not just the God of the hills; He is God of the valleys. God specializes in helping us when and where we need it the most—in life's valleys.

In the valley, Satan wants to break us, but God wants to make us. Be strong! You are still a "hyper-conqueror," even, and especially, in your weakest moment. That is where we discover that the Jesus in us really is greater than he that is in the world. Jesus really is the answer, even when we still have some questions—questions like:

- "What about the hurts I have suffered in the valley?"
- "Can God use me again after all I've been through?"
- "Why am I going through such a difficult time?"
- "What do I do when I feel like giving up?"

We will talk about each of these questions in the coming chapters.

Chapter 2

Valleys of
Our Own Mistakes

I am a movie buff, a love passed on to me by my mother. Sometimes I think it is more of a vice than a virtue, especially considering some of the stuff that comes out of Hollywood these days. Still, movies can be for me a source of escape and entertainment. But one thing bothers me about most movies: They never show consequences for actions.

In the movies cars can jump hundreds of feet over obstacles without popping a tire or causing any other severe damage. I barely brushed a curb the other day and had to spend several hundred dollars to repair the rim and buy a new tire. In the movies our heroes escape from one life-threatening situation after another, dodging bullets and scarcely messing up their hair. In real life I am just glad to finish shaving without severing an artery. In short, the movies often portray an unreal kind of life where choices are without typical consequences.

I would like to see, just once, a James Bond film in which Agent 007 has to confess that due to all of his sexual exploits he has contracted the AIDS virus, or perhaps a less-threatening sexually transmitted disease. I would like to see one of his many beautiful world-class lovers pushing a two-year-old around the block in a stroller, a lasting and living reminder of her one-night stand with the super secret agent.

But does Hollywood show that side of life? Rarely. We only get to see the car chases, the steamy love scenes and the narrow escapes—all without the consequences that real life brings. It's all play, no consequences.

Most people have heard of John Wesley, the founder of the Methodist Church. He and his brother, Charles, were used by God to turn around an entire nation, England, in the 1700s. In Christian history, few names stand out like John Wesley's. He was a great man, a fiery preacher and clearly blessed by God.

But he wasn't living on a movie screen. Wesley, like all of us, made some unwise choices that had long-lasting and negative ramifications. Just a couple of days after becoming engaged to Molly Vazeille, a wealthy widow, Wesley slipped on ice on London Bridge and was taken to her home to recuperate. A week later, unable to travel to his meetings, Wesley and Vazeille married.

Within a few months after their marriage, the jealous disposition of his wife troubled Wesley. She misconstrued the affectionate language Wesley used in writing to women involved in the founding of the Methodist Church. And as the fires of jealousy burned, coupled with her inability to cope with the time and devotion required by the burgeoning Methodist movement, she left him.[1] Some even say it was not uncommon for her to disrupt Wesley's meetings, sometimes publicly accusing him of being a liar and a cheat. She became notorious for her antics and difficult behavior.

Why would God allow one of his greatest servants to walk through such a valley?

Wesley really should have known better. His own mother, Susanna, was truly a saint. She not only birthed and nurtured more than sixteen children, but she also "home schooled" them, teaching not simply reading, writing and arithmetic, but Latin, Greek, basic theology and the Bible. Talk about your well-rounded skillful woman! It is said that in order to get some devotional time for herself she would take her outer skirt (women wore lots of undergarments in those days) and lift it over her head. Her kids were so well trained that when they saw her do this, they knew it was time to be quiet and leave her alone.

The bottom line is that even a great saint like John Wesley could not escape the consequences of his own decisions. God did not stick him in what seemed like the marriage from hell. Wesley put himself there. He simply did what we all do sometimes—make a quick decision that seems right at the time but ends up having long-term negative results. Did this unfortunate decision stop Wesley from preaching, evangelizing and fulfilling his destiny? Absolutely not. He pressed on, and the world still looks to him as one of the great figures of British and Christian history.

Valleys come at all of us from all directions. Some come our way because of the mistakes we have made. Others hit us because of what somebody else has done. It is one thing to have to sleep in a bed we made for ourselves; it is quite another thing to go through a grueling time because of what someone else has done. Still other valleys in our lives seem random and cruel because we do not know where they come from or whom to blame. No matter where or from whom they come, valleys hurt and can bring the best of us to tears.

In Psalm 84:5–6 we find the Valley of Baca, meaning "tears." Surprisingly, those passing through the valley of tears are not the weak, the rebels or the troubled. Rather, they are those who are pursuing God.

> Blessed are those whose strength is in you,
>> who have set their hearts on pilgrimage.
> As they pass through the Valley of Baca,
>> they make it a place of springs;
>> the autumn rains also cover it with pools.
>
> —PSALM 84:5–6

Every pilgrimage starts with a promise and ends with a provision. But between the promise and the provision is a problem—sometimes a valley of tears. Whether we are on a detour because, like John Wesley, we made a hasty decision concerning an important life issue, or whether we are still on the right tract pursing God, a time of weeping may await us before we reach our destination. At one time or another, every one of us will walk through the valley of tears. The Old Testament declares a season for weeping as well as rejoicing. In the New Testament we are commanded to weep with those who weep. There is nothing unspiritual about having tears in our eyes as we go through a tough time. The promise of the psalmist is that God will see us through the valley—turning our tears into springs of joy and pools of delight.

CHOICES

It was widely reported in 1991 that Wayne McLaren, a former male model who once portrayed the "Marlboro Man," sued his physician for not diagnosing his lung cancer early enough to be treated. McLaren had smoked more than a pack of cigarettes a day for twenty-five years, and yet it seemed he was blaming his doctor for his condition.[2]

Playing the "blame game" seems to have become a favorite American pastime—when the going gets tough, never look in the mirror; instead, find someone to point an accusing finger at.

The Bible has a different take. Galatians 6:7 says, "Do not be deceived: God cannot be mocked. A man reaps what he sows." If the physical universe operates by cause and effect, the moral universe operates by choice and consequence. Let's be honest; much of the hard times we go through in life are the direct or indirect result of choices we have made in our "yesterdays." Everybody wants to experience a better life, but few are truly willing to make the necessary changes. It is easier to blame other people or God for the troubles we are experiencing. Thus, it is someone else's responsibility to change. Every parent knows what it is like to get blamed by a teenage son or daughter for "ruining" their life.

A few years back, an overweight convicted drug possessor in Arizona claimed he did not receive a fair trial because there were no obese people on the jury. His conviction was not due to his own actions, so he claimed, but rather to an unsympathetic jury.[3] Like many convicted criminals, he was still blaming "the system" even though he was the one who had committed the crime. It is easier to claim the system needs fixing than to work on fixing ourselves.

I read about a college professor who was fired for sexually harassing a teenage female student. He demanded that the school give him his job back and claimed that he was handicapped, as defined by state law, and suffered from "a handicap of sexual addiction." Thankfully, his reinstatement was denied.[4]

While I applaud the terrific work that has been done in the area of recovery, I must confess I get nervous about calling all of our personal problems a "disease" or "dysfunction." If such an approach leads to help and healing—great. But if and when it leads to shirking responsibility and playing the "blame game," then something is wrong. Even someone with a physical disease or dysfunction, such as cancer, should have the sense to take enough responsibility to get to a doctor for help.

Bad choices yield bad results, no matter whom we try to blame. Walking through a mess we created for ourselves is one of the most difficult valleys we can go through. The valley of tears that results from the guilt and grief over our own bad choices captures many people, never letting them go. Every person on the planet has to walk through this valley at one time or another, for feelings of guilt and shame are universal. It is not just religious people who experience guilt; it is everybody. Shame and guilt are not simply the imposition of the religious establishment; they are the result of ignoring a "warning light" inside every human being.

Concerning those who do not have the benefits of the law of God, Paul said, "They show that the requirements of the law are written on their hearts, their consciences also bearing witness, and their thoughts now accusing, now even defending them" (Rom. 2:15). So the problem with always blaming someone or something else for our difficulties is that it does not satisfy the demands of our own conscience. Conscience is like a tagalong brother that we cannot get rid of—no matter how many sitcoms we watch to drown it out, how many women we date, how much alcohol we drink or how much money we make. God's law is written on our hearts, and we intrinsically know that somehow, some way, we have violated it.

Nothing destroys a soul faster than guilt. I have seen it happen time and time again, leading otherwise productive Christians into serious regret, shame, frustration and depression. When guilt takes hold, we become fixated on past sins and mistakes. We began to live life in the rearview mirror—no longer seeing life's opportunities before us because we are blinded by a past full of what "would have been, could have been and should have been."

When we allow a guilty conscience to ascend the throne of our heart, we become subject to a tyrant. I am reminded of the famous scene in Shakespeare's *Macbeth* when Lady Macbeth, a kind of Jezebel of her day, was sleepwalking and saying, "Out, damned spot," her mind haunted by guilt and the blood of the king she and her husband conspired to murder.

In a way, all of us have a Lady Macbeth lurking in our conscience. We all have dark spots in our past. The Bible word for this, of course, is *sin.* And it is not just murder that can cause us problems. James says in his New Testament letter:

> If you really keep the royal law found in Scripture, "Love your neighbor as yourself," you are doing right. But if you show favoritism, you sin and are convicted by the law as lawbreakers. For whoever keeps the whole law and yet stumbles at just one point is guilty of breaking all of it. For he who said, "Do not commit adultery," also said, "Do not murder." If you do not commit adultery but you do commit murder, you have become a lawbreaker.
>
> —JAMES 2:8–11

In other words, telling a little white lie is as much a sin as killing somebody, even though murder is a more serious act. We do not have to commit the so-called serious sins to be ravaged by guilt. To misquote an old commercial slogan, *A little sin will do ya.*

Have you ever heard anyone say that all sin is alike? Actually, this is both true and false. Sin is a condition we are in, a state we are in, before it is an act or deed we commit. Before we do something wrong, say something wrong or think something wrong, there is something wrong inside of us. Little acts of sin committed by a child are symptoms of an internal condition, as are severe acts committed by hardened criminals. All sin is sin, from the young child lying about having that cookie to the atrocities of a serial killer. All acts of sin are the same in that they proceed from the same internal condition of separation from God.

But does it follow, then, that no one sin is better or worse than any other act of sin? No. In the Old Testament, certain acts of sin required a more serious penalty than others. Common sense tells us that you do not take a child who has lied and execute him, nor do you take a murderer like Ted Bundy and slap him on the wrist and send him to his room. Some sinful acts are indeed worse than other sinful acts.

Before being tempted to think, however, that we do not need help from God or anyone else because we are not as bad as someone else, we must remember that all of us remain sinners. One person may have a worse case of terminal cancer than we have, but cancer is still deadly if not properly dealt with. Besides that, even though our symptoms are not as terrible as somebody else's, unless we deal with the root cause our symptoms may worsen.

Many Christians think they are in less need of grace than others, but given the right (or perhaps wrong) chance, any one of us could become the most abject of sinners. I have read stories of some of the people who became leaders in Hitler's Third Reich. To the outward eye they were not stupid, ignorant or particularly evil. Some of them had prestigious university degrees and held places of honor in decent society—they were men who should have known better than to have joined in the atrocities of the Nazis.

In the book *Lord of the Flies,* the author makes a similar point. He took a bunch of proper English kids, shipwrecked them on an island and told the story of how depraved these previously well-behaved children became. At the time of the book's publication, England was expanding its kingdom all around the world, and stories of "savages" from remote conquered lands were quite popular. Few in Great Britain would have considered the possibility of having any savage nature in them. *Lord of the Flies* was written to proper England to show that if you put anybody, no matter how spotless, in a certain situation, you might get gut-turning results.

Sin is choosing self over God. Sin is humankind's "Declaration of Independence" against the Creator. To illustrate the nature and effect of sin I would compare it to a scuba diver with an air tank on his back and tubes connecting that air to his mouth. Imagine the diver going down into the coral reefs, taking his time, relaxing and breathing normally as he watches a rainbow of fish swim by. Then a beautiful, brilliant-colored sea serpent swims up and says, "What's going on? Are you enjoying the view?"

The diver says, "I am having so much fun. It's like a whole new world down here."

The serpent says, "You haven't seen anything. There is a whole other dimension of living, but you can only partially experience it with that tank on your back. Who told you to put that tank on your back?"

"The guide told me that when I go under I should put this tank on my back because if I don't, I'll die from lack of oxygen."

"That guy is lying. He doesn't want you to be free. Look around! Do you see any of us down here with tanks on our backs? No. It's that guide—he wants you to be dependent on him, but I am telling you, if you want to experience all this life has to offer, you have to get rid of that tank. Be free and do whatever you want."

So the diver throws the tank off and discovers that what the serpent said is true. Sure enough, he is free. He can do what he wants, when he wants and without encumbrance. He goes inside caves and coral reefs that were inaccessible with the tank on. He sees fish that never come into the open areas. He feels alive in a new way—the adrenaline is pumping, and a whole new dimension of life has begun.

But he soon discovers, rather too late, that the sea serpent had not told him the whole truth. The moment he tries to take a breath, he realizes there is no air source. The tank is long gone, and the coral reefs for all their beauty offer no oxygen. Without getting plugged back into the air source, he will die.

That is true of us. We are lured in by sin's beauty, but the moment we need peace, joy or true love, we are sucking water. We have been thrilled, but now the thrill is gone. We are unplugged. We are dying.

This death is part of the human condition, because all of us are rebels wanting to "do our own thing," even if we are not outwardly sinning in an obvious way. In the Sermon on the Mount, Jesus made a statement over and over: "You have heard it said...But I say to you..." He applied it to anger, adultery, forgiveness and more. In every one of those statements He was taking sin beyond the specific act back to the source—He was following the rope into the cave and showing us where it began. He was making the point that even if we could control ourselves and keep from sinning in a particular area, there was still a sin problem on the inside waiting to break out, perhaps in another area.

Inside each of us is some area, or two or three, where we are weak. Maybe you have a problem with drinking, hating people of other races or envying your neighbor's possessions or his wife. Even if you keep from drinking, making bigoted remarks or eyeing your neighbor's possessions and wife, sin still is active on the inside, and it can pop out in another quarter—sometimes at the most awkward times.

FALSE GUILT

When we enter a valley that we have brought on ourselves, whether in unabashed disobedience to God or in simple ignorance or blatant stupidity, we can come under the burden of guilt. Even mature believers can be bound by guilt. The lack of liberty and joy in their Christian walk is easily detected.

Sad to say, the church is often a major manufacturer of false or illegitimate guilt. Religion of any kind tends to be a great guilt imposer. I grew up in a somewhat fundamentalist church where you didn't, as they say, "smoke, drink, chew or go with girls that do." Many churches have what I call the "Big Five Test" for holiness: Don't smoke, drink, dance, play cards or go to the theater. Some churches preach against all five. Others specialize in preaching against two or three. To this day I am not much of a dancer because I was taught that dancing is wrong. I tease our congregation that if they ever see me swaying to the praise and worship music, then they better know that the Holy Spirit has fallen, for that is major dancing for me!

Now I do not recommend or condone smoking or drinking as an acceptable Christian lifestyle, but neither do I believe that these superficial issues are at the core of true holiness. Superficial religious guilt can lead us to major on minors. For example, I remember good Christians who thought President Nixon was an unfairly beleaguered president, despite mounting evidence of serious abuse of power, until the Watergate tapes came out replete with "expletives deleted." In other words, the president was caught on tape swearing. The cussing bothered them more than the crimes Nixon was accused of committing. Why? Because it violated their religious perception of holiness.

I remember one of the early leaders in the charismatic church sharing that he was raised to believe that movies were inherently sinful. The first movie he ever went to was *The Sound of Music*. If Hollywood has ever produced a wholesome film to take the whole family to see, it has to be *The Sound of Music*. Yet he confessed that he felt like a vile sinner as he sneaked in, not unlike a guy trying to slip unnoticed into a sleazy X-rated theater. He did not want to be seen. The adrenaline was flowing. His heart was thumping. He sat low in his seat and watched Julie Andrews singing as she twirled around the Austrian Alps. It was a far cry from the wicked experience he had been led to expect. Some valleys are unnecessary!

Religion can certainly impose false guilt, but that does not mean that all guilt is artificial. Skeptics are quick to point out flaws in the church's teaching, but they are not so anxious to acknowledge the many true and life-giving principles she provides.

God is not some "cosmic kill-joy" looking down from heaven busy creating laws to bother us. It is not as if He sees us having fun committing adultery or lying, and so just to bug us He declares, "Thou shalt not commit adultery. Thou shalt not lie." Not at all. Every principle and law of God, untainted by religious interpretation, is given to maximize our enjoyment of the life He has so graciously conferred upon us. True guilt then, not self-imposed or religion-inflicted shame, is actually positive in that it serves as a warning that something is wrong and needs to be corrected. God has given us some clear principles to bless our lives—not to bind us, but to loose us. When we break those principles, we feel legitimate guilt.

We try to deal with guilt in different ways.

Often we flat-out deny it—"I didn't do anything wrong." Like an alcoholic refusing to admit he has a problem, we refuse to accept any responsibility for our own actions. Or we attempt to rid ourselves of guilt by getting rid of the supposed cause of that guilt—the standard we have been taught by the church, society or government. "You can't impose your morality on me," we say. "Different strokes for different folks. That may be your idea of right and wrong, but mine is different."

Then, when we still feel the guilt, we try to forget about it. "Shake it off! Don't let it bother you anymore. Move on in life."

Then we want to minimize it. "It's not that big of a deal. It won't really hurt anyone. I know lots of people who have done the same thing."

Have you ever noticed that the enemy minimizes sin and guilt before we fall and maximizes it afterward? "Come on, cheat on the test. How do you think people get through school? It's no big deal." So you cheat. But after you have done it, he comes back singing a different tune, "Never in the history of humankind has anyone made a bigger mistake than you did." We feel like saying, "Wait a minute! Where were you before? I thought you said it was no big deal." Still, we are prone to believe the voice of condemnation because our own hearts accuse us.

Another way to avoid guilt is to commit the sin again and again so the conscience becomes seared, no longer feeling the discomfort of guilt. Ask anyone, from a habitual liar or cheater to a death-row murderer—the first offense is always harder than the rest. Soon the heart does not even flinch when the sin is committed. The apostle Paul noted that in the last days this approach would become increasingly common, as "hypocritical liars" would sear their consciences "with a hot iron." (See 1 Timothy 4:2.)

Some people pile wrong choices on top of wrong choices. I read about a man who was bitten by a rattlesnake while trying to kiss it. In a panic, he tried to break down the venom by attaching his tongue to a 6-volt battery, and ended up losing one lip and part of his tongue.[5]

Another man dropped his keys into a portable toilet by accident. He made it worse when he climbed down into the toilet, after removing his shoes and pants, to look for them and became stuck. He was rescued an hour and a half later after nearby children heard his cries for help. Doctors had to remove the toilet seat, which had become wedged around his torso.[6]

While stories like this make us laugh, the results of dealing with a guilty conscience by searing it with repeated sin are not so funny. Just ask any addict who is going through the pain of attempted recovery. It is not so easy, and it definitely is not funny.

Sometimes we try to blame others for our sin, as if we could take the boxes of guilt out of our own spiritual closet and put them in someone else's. "My dad was this way, so I really had no choice. It runs in the family." I am sure each of us could think of a thousand and one reasons why someone else deserves more blame for our sin than we do.

There was a young woman who used to attend our church whose father had left her mother at a certain age. All we heard from this woman was that her husband would certainly leave her when she reached that age. As she drew close to that age she began to transform herself into a horrible, nagging, impossible woman who literally drove her husband out—fulfilling what she had been saying for years. The very thing she feared the most had come upon her—a self-fulfilled prophecy. Yet if you asked her who was to blame for her divorce, she would point her finger at her parents.

Still another way we deal with guilt is to beat ourselves with it. This is, sadly, the method many Christians use to deal with guilt, and they get stuck in the valley of tears, mourning their own imperfections. "I'm worthless. I'm stupid. I'm morally inferior. I don't deserve God. I don't deserve another chance," they say, as if heaping up sacrifices will somehow assuage their offended conscience.

Satan does not care what trap he gets you in. If he cannot keep you from confessing your sins, he will keep you confessing them over and over and over again. As a Roman Catholic priest, Martin Luther would literally whip himself because he could not live up to God's standards. This was a common practice in his day. Like so many others ravaged by guilt, he was trying to pay the price for the sin he committed.

How barbaric that may seem to us in this present day. But before we are too quick to condemn a past generation, maybe we need to remember that people still do the same thing today. Not literally, but emotionally. A lot of us whip ourselves on the inside. The enemy accuses us, and we agree with him, forgetting about grace. Some of us are so used to beating ourselves up that we do not feel that we have been to church unless the pastor whips us and makes us feel small and dirty. In a perverted way, we feel that the whipping brings cleansing. Some altars are full of self-flagellation every Sunday morning.

My experience has convinced me that many believers do not have a good self-image, so we are susceptible to the ongoing ravages of guilt. We sabotage ourselves when we are at the brink of success. Subconsciously we do not think we deserve a good life full of God's blessings. We cannot live up to our own standards, much less God's.

Luther knew what that was like. He was reading the Book of Romans one day and came across this passage:

> Therefore no one will be declared righteous in his sight by observing the law; rather, through the law we become conscious of sin. But now a righteousness from God, apart from law, has been made known, to which the Law and the Prophets testify. This righteousness from God comes through faith in Jesus Christ to all who believe. There is no difference, for all have sinned and fall short of the glory of God, and are justified freely by his grace through the redemption that came by Christ Jesus.
> —ROMANS 3:20–24

Suddenly, a light flashed in Luther's mind. He began to understand that he could do nothing to add to the grace God had already given him, and this epiphany changed the course of his life—and of history.

Paul says in Ephesians 2:8, "For it is by grace you have been saved, through faith—this not from yourselves, it is the gift of God—not by works, so that no one can boast."

Grace is unmerited favor, getting something we do not deserve. Some have used an acronym for grace: God's Riches At Christ's Expense.

Before grace, we were all drowning in deep waters that we got ourselves into. There were no lifeguards, no buoys and no passing rafts. We had thrown off the oxygen tank and were doomed, but then God threw us a "Jesus preserver." We did not earn it, and we did not ask for it. We may have even been hurt and bitter, cursing God at the time. But all we had to do by faith was embrace that Jesus preserver and we were saved—no self-flagellation necessary.

While we are busy beating ourselves with guilt, God is working to move us out of the pit of self-pity and onto the stage of destiny. This is why God saves us. We are not simply saved *from,* but saved *for.* God did not simply bring Israel *out* of the land of Egypt, but *into* the Promised Land. God wants to bring us out of our valleys for a purpose.

After noting we are saved by grace, Paul goes on to say, "For we are God's workmanship" (v. 10). *Workmanship* is the Greek word *poema,* from which we get the English word *poem.* You and I are God's unique, special poem. God has never written a poem quite like you, nor will He again. All of us are "one of a kind" and irreplaceable in the eyes of God.

Poema was used of a journeyman who went through several levels of training until he became a master craftsman; the last step before becoming a master craftsman was to produce a masterpiece, much like students today write a thesis to get a Ph.D., or pass written and oral exams.

Did you know that you are God's masterpiece? You are His Pulitzer Prize-winning poem. Guilt makes us forget that. God knows more about you than you know about yourself. He knows you on your best and your worst days. And you know what? He still loves you and believes you have potential. It is by grace you have been saved through faith. It is not your own doing. It is the gift of God—a gift given by someone who knows what you did in the past.

When guilt comes calling, we do not feel like a masterpiece. We hear ourselves thinking, *Shame on you! How could I have done such a thing?* The answer to the fiery darts of guilt and the inner voices of shame is found at the cross. The cross is where God ultimately and finally took our guilt and shame away and demonstrated His love. Knowing how to apply the power of the cross to even our freshest and most humiliating sins is the key to making it through the valley of tears.

I remember hearing the story about a man who in the

early part of the last century was an electrical wizard for General Electric, which is to this day one of the largest corporations in the world. They were a fast-growing company back then, and the man had been their resident genius for years before he finally retired. One day, not long after his retirement, the story goes, an entire complex of important machinery broke down at a main GE plant. Try as they might, the engineers there could not figure out what the problem was. They finally said, "Let's give him a call. He is still around someplace. He'll probably come back and help us solve the problem."

He did indeed come down and had them turn on every big complex of machines they could turn on; then he walked in between these huge machines and listened. Without saying a word he scrutinized every sight and sound. Soon he walked up to a particular machine, took out of his coat a piece of chalk, made a cross mark on a particular spot on the machine and said, "Men, right in there is where you will find your problem." Then he went home. To their utter amazement, when they opened up that piece of machinery, right there at that spot, they found the problem. They fixed it and got the plant back in operation.

A few weeks later they received an invoice from the recently retired man. It was for $10,000—an incredible sum of money at the time. The higher-ups at GE were angry. They said, "How long was he here?"

"Just a few moments."

"What did he do?"

"Just made his cross mark and left."

"You better find out why he is trying to bill $10,000 for just a few moments of work."

So they sent him a request to itemize his invoice. He sent them back a now famous two-line, itemized invoice:

Cost of chalk, $1.00
Knowing where to put the cross mark, $9,999.00
Total, $10,000.00

They paid the invoice.[7]

Do you know where to put the cross? Has the complex machinery that is your life broken down? The good news is that believers have a resident expert inside who will never retire, and the Holy Spirit is willing and able to guide us through the valley of tears, applying the power of the cross wherever necessary. Guilt then becomes nothing more than an indicator that the cross needs to be put where our sin was. And if feelings of guilt remain after we have been forgiven, then we need to apply the cross there too, for it is a cross of grace.

RELENTLESS GUILT

Some people know that they have been forgiven and that the cross has been applied, but they still feel the weight of guilt. I believe there are two reasons for this.

First, the person may not have genuinely repented. Sorrow for sin and repentance from sin are two different things. People may really feel sorry for sinning and know it was wrong, but for whatever reason they may not yet have decided to change their ways. In that case, God is still going after your heart, and He will allow the conscience to continue telling you that what you are doing is wrong. This is the healthy function of guilt: to turn saint and sinner alike to their Savior that He may unburden them. If you feel haunted by guilt, ask yourself if you have really given up the sin: "Am I just sorry for my sin, or have I repented from my sin?"

Paul told the Corinthians he was not too upset that his first letter had caused them to feel bad, for hurt feelings are only temporary and can become the springboard for repentance. "Godly sorrow brings repentance that leads to salvation and leaves no regret, but worldly sorrow brings death" (2 Cor. 7:10).

The second reason for relentless feelings of guilt is that we face a real enemy who is constantly accusing us. I grew up hearing this phrase, "The devil brings condemnation, but God brings conviction." This is one important way my Sunday school teachers taught me to distinguish between the voice of God and the voice of the devil. The devil condemns, trying to make us feel worthless and broken.

The hallmark of condemnation is the feeling that there is no hope. On the other hand, the Holy Spirit brings conviction. The accompanying feelings can still be heavy, but God's conviction always contains the seeds of promise and freedom. The conviction of Christ is full of hope. Condemnation says we are worthless; conviction says we can do better. Learning the difference between condemnation—which should never be accepted, even if it comes through a well-intentioned fellow Christian or preacher—and conviction—which is a life-giving rebuke—will spare us from swallowing any more of the enemy's poison.

When we are in the valley of tears, the voice of condemnation wants to keep us there. The devil says, "Run away; hide. Don't go near church until you get your act together. Go at least three days without smoking, and then you can go to church and be forgiven. Try to go six days without looking at pornography, and then talk to God about forgiveness." We are tempted to think we must clean up own act, on our own power, before even considering asking God for help. "You're too dirty for God."

Such thinking quickly becomes an endless downward spiral. We try to get good enough on our own, which of course we cannot do, and we end up with ever-increasing pangs of guilt and shame. If we are to ever make it out of the valley of tears, all such thinking must be totally rejected. We must apply the cross to our hurts and shame, throwing ourselves into the arms of grace. Jesus is the answer even before we have the slightest clue how to get ourselves out of mess we are in. First John 1:9 says, "If we confess our sins, he is faithful and just and will forgive us our sins and purify us from all unrighteousness." Almost sounds too easy and too good to be true, doesn't it? That is why the gospel means "good news."

Why worry about a bill that has already been paid? Jesus on the cross said, "It is finished," which in the Greek means "paid in full." Talk about easy payments! How about no payments? Nobody worries about making payments on a car or a house after they have paid for it. If someone questions you, you produce the pink slip or title deed to prove it. What you do not have to do is make more payments simply to prove to the inquisitors that the car is really yours.

In the same manner, believers do not have to keep begging for mercy and forgiveness over and over again when challenged by guilt and shame. When the devil questions whether you are saved or forgiven, you can produce the blood-stained receipt that Christ paid for us on the cross. On that receipt are stamped the words *PAID IN FULL.* That receipt can become our ticket out of the valley of tears.

In the Book of Lamentations, Jeremiah points out that in the midst of the most severe trials God's love is constant. His love is like a fountain of water that cannot be plugged up, clogged up or damned up. No matter what we do to try to stop it, it just keeps flowing toward us.

One morning before church my wife, running late as usual, was rushing to get dressed and out of the house. As Marguerite was attempting to turn off the bath water, the handle broke off with the water still running. What a time for this to happen! I was already gone, and she didn't know what to do. Water was gushing all over the place, and her best attempts to keep the tub from overflowing and ruining our house were failing. For a while she took a bucket and tried to keep up with the flow by throwing the water out the window, but the water level kept rising. Finally, in desperation she ran and got our next door neighbor, who calmly turned off the water main.

That picture of water, water, water, unstoppable in its flow, is a perfect image of the love and grace of God. And, unlike our house, there is no main valve to turn it off. You can ignore, reject or run from God's love, but you cannot stop it from flowing toward you. Putting your finger up the faucet to stop the flow of water is a futile exercise. So is trying to escape the power of God's love. You can curse God, yell at God and say, "God, I don't want anything to do with You!" God just keeps flowing with love.

It is this unconditional, unstoppable flow of God's love that finally captures our hearts. The deepest, darkest and driest valleys can be turned into conduits of the grace and power of His stubborn love. Even when we are walking through a mess that we created for ourselves, grace keeps the flow of divine love coming our way. Finally, we cannot help but concur with the words of that grand hymn, "Amazing grace! How sweet the sound, that saved a wretch like me! I once was lost, but now am found, was blind, but now I see."[8]

This is the essence and heart of the gospel. God's grace was never meant to co-rule with self-condemnation. We are not motivated by guilt, but by grace. What we could not do for ourselves, God did for us, not so that we would whip ourselves with guilt, but so that we would be free. That is the only way to get rid of guilt and to be cleansed on the inside. Do not beg, bribe or bargain with God. That is simply a subtle form of pride—as if you have something to offer in return for His grace. Humbly receive it and have confidence that nagging guilt is not meant to be part of the Christian life.

AFTER THE SIN

David's sexual escapade with Bathsheba is infamous. One spring evening while strolling on the rooftop the king saw a UFO—an Unclad Female Object. She was beautiful, he was the king, and so without thinking of the consequences, he had her brought to him so he could sleep with her. Well, as we have seen, choices have consequences, and David soon discovered the magnitude of the mess he had led himself and others into. Not only was she now pregnant with his child, but she was married to one of David's best generals, Uriah.

David realized his sin might be exposed, but instead of immediately repenting and dealing with the mistake in a godly fashion, he hatched a plan to cover his sin. He would have Uriah come home from the battlefield for a little R and R, expecting during this time for him to sleep with his wife, Bathsheba, thus making it plausible that the child she was carrying belonged to her husband. But when Uriah refused to sleep with his wife out of allegiance to the other men who were still fighting the battle, David went further into deception. He had Uriah placed on the front lines and instructed his other men to pull back, allowing Uriah to die at the hands of the enemy.

Talk about a cover-up! Watergate and the Monica Lewinsky scandal are really not all that new. The plot is as scandalous as many Hollywood movies: lust, deception, drunkenness, treachery and murder. All of this at the hands of David, God's chosen man who suddenly found himself in the web of sin. In David's defense, however, it must be noted that in time he did do the right thing.

We do not know what David's conscience was telling him for all those weeks and months, but God had a prophet in the land, Nathan, who confronted him about the sin. Only after being exposed did David repent. He should have made things right much earlier, but at least he did the right thing in the end. And no matter how much you have messed up your life, perhaps even piling one mess upon another, there is still time for you to get things right. During his time of repentance David wrote Psalm 51:

> Create in me a clean heart, O God....Do not take Your Holy Spirit from me....Restore to me the joy of Your salvation.
>
> —PSALM 51:10–12, NKJV

As David learned, some things will not go away by pretending, denying or lying. The first step in getting out of the valley of tears is to acknowledge our sin and need of grace. It is not enough to be sorry—we must be ready to repent. Even then, there may be consequences we have to live with for awhile.

In David's case, the baby he had fathered was born to Bathsheba, but God had spoken through the prophet Nathan that the baby would die. Sure enough, immediately following the birth, the baby became gravely ill. David interceded for the child with all his might. He took off his kingly clothes and put on sackcloth, a sign of mourning and repentance. Then he lay prostrate before the Lord day and night, pleading for mercy. I can almost hear him crying out, "O God, it's not fair! It's my sin. If you want to take someone, take me! Don't take out Your wrath on my innocent little baby." He refused to eat or be consoled in any fashion. His servants and advisors could only watch and shake their heads. Despite his most fervent intercession, the child died.

This hit David hard. It was his sin that had killed not just one person, but two: Uriah and the baby. I can only imagine the guilt that must have dogged him. The giant-killer, the lion-slayer, the anointed one of God had become a murderer, liar and adulterer. He was at one of the lowest points in his life.

But David did something remarkable. He did not let his guilt run him in circles. He made several choices I think are key if we are to walk out of the valley we have created by our own bad choices.

Get up.

A season of mourning is healthy, but an overextended season of grief becomes a pity party. Pain is inevitable, but prolonged misery is not. When you keep your guilt alive, you focus more on your sin than on grace, and that goes against God's plan.

David got up, washed himself, went to church and worshiped God. Then he went home and had a feast. This confused his servants, who wanted to know why there had been such a remarkable turnaround, but in reality, David was doing something spiritually healthy. He was getting back into a routine of living, despite the feelings that may have still plagued his heart. Getting up and dusting ourselves off is the first step in leaving our bad choices behind.

David changed his focus. Here's what he told his servants who were confused by his sudden change:

> While the child was still alive, I fasted and I wept. I thought, "Who knows? The LORD may be gracious to me and let the child live." But now that he is dead, why should I fast? Can I bring him back again? I will go to him, but he will not return to me.
>
> —2 SAMUEL 12:22

Accept what cannot be changed.

David recognized that the past could not be changed. He had sinned, and the baby had been lost. Now what? Should he build an altar to his guilty conscience? Should he wake up every day and try to win God's favor back? No. A guilty conscience can do nothing to remit past sin.

I occasionally hear of churches that have put bodies in caskets in front of the church because someone had a spurious word from God that the deceased would be raised from the dead. Although I never want to get in the way of what God wants to do by way of miracles, serious damage has been done to churches and to sincere Christians because a few overzealous people will not accept what cannot and should not be changed.

David was a man who had seen God do great miracles, but he also knew when to accept that which could not be changed. Again, pain is inevitable; misery is optional.

Play it down and pray it up.

David did not maximize the problem—he maximized God. He did not drape himself over the child's grave and weep day after day. He went to church and worshiped God. God not only has the solution—He is the solution!

When you are stuck in a cycle of self-condemnation—pray. Do not tell Him how bad you are; tell Him how good He is. Change the direction of your thoughts from inward to outward. Pray harder than you have ever prayed. Worship more than you have ever worshiped. Let praise flow from your lips. Give your mind something to dwell on other than thoughts of your own guilt. Not enough can be said for the value of prayer in the time of heartache. It cleanses like a pure stream.

Focus on what is left, not on what is lost.

Though you may have lost many things—relationships,

career, respect, ministry and/or money—because of bad choices, there is always something left with which to work. In David's case, he had a country to run, battles to fight and a woman—Bathsheba—who needed his love and comfort. The Bible says David did comfort Bathsheba. We know he did more than that because nine months later she gave birth to another child—Solomon, the next king of Israel.

Yes, a child had been taken from them, but God also gave them a new baby and put a new plan in that baby's heart. If David had continued grieving for the one that had been lost, he might have messed up the plan God had for Solomon. Imagine being Solomon and growing up in the shadow of the baby your father lost due to an illicit affair. Imagine your dad moping around the house, bummed over his own failure to hit the mark. That could have been Solomon's situation had David focused on what was lost rather than what was left.

What we have lost can never be regained, but that does not mean that everything is lost forever. God has something more, and the new may well be better than the old we are grieving over. As Paul said in Philippians 3:13–14, "But one thing I do: Forgetting what is behind and straining toward what is ahead, I press on." That is what David did and what we should do—press on!

THE BEST CHOICE

Some of you are stuck in the valley of tears because you have not reconciled with and moved beyond your own bad choices. You are surrounded by shattered dreams and dashed hopes. You wonder how you could have done what you did, hurt the people you hurt and inflicted wounds on yourself.

Take heart! God has forgiven you. He remembers your sin no more and wants you to move out of this valley. When your heart is full of grace, there will be no room for guilt.

Chapter 3

Valleys Others
Put Us Through

She was in her eighties when I first saw her in what was an old movie theater in Fullerton, California—this Dutch woman who had became so well known and adored by people in the twentieth-century church. I was only in my early twenties, but I had already been privileged to study under some of the greatest Christian minds in academia: men with two and three Ph.D.'s from such prestigious universities as Harvard, Oxford and Cambridge. I had seen the greatest preachers of the day strut the stage and pound the pulpit. But what I learned from that old lady dwarfed what I had been taught anywhere else, because she spoke not with mere human learning or superior intellectual reasoning, but rather with an authority that can only come from God.

Corrie ten Boom had been a young woman living in Amsterdam in the early 1900s, a woman in love with a man and expecting the things from life we all look forward to: a husband, a family, a peaceful home, grandchildren. But the man she thought she would marry betrayed her and married someone else, leaving her single in a day when being unmarried after a certain age was considered abnormal, especially if you were female.

By the time World War II came, Corrie was what the world might call a middle-aged spinster. She, her father and her sister, Betsie, watched as the persecution against the Jews grew stronger, and when the Nazis took over Amsterdam, she and her family made the courageous decision to hide Jews in the hopes of shielding them from certain imprisonment and probable death. This they did until betrayed by a friend. Consequently, both the Jews they had been hiding and Corrie's entire family were thrown into the horrors of a concentration camp.

The decision of the ten Boom family to protect Jews from the tyranny of the Nazis proved costly. Corrie's father, gravely ill, a situation acerbated by the conditions of the camp, was released, only to die days later. Her sister, Betsie, died in the camp only weeks before liberation. Corrie herself was released by accident a few weeks before the Allied Forces came. She found out later that the Nazis had given a specific order to execute her, but that order somehow got confused, and she was released.

When she had lived in the concentration camp, Corrie had been prone to anger and bitterness. Why was God allowing this to happen to them, a good Christian family? Had they not been doing His will hiding His chosen people from Nazi abuse? Why hadn't God protected them? Her sister, however, had a different spirit. Betsie would wake up every morning with praise on her lips. She seemed unmoved by her awful surroundings, and she would not only thank God for each new day, but for little things—even the daily annoyances of life in the camp.

"Praise God for the bedbugs, Corrie," she would say, "for at least we have a bed." At the time, Corrie could not decide if her sister's attitude was encouraging, irritating or just plain stupid. Her sister's spirit did, at any rate, keep her going when she felt she could not go on. Years later, Corrie's eyes would sparkle as she recalled to us that after being released she found out that the women in her cabin had not been raped by the guards for one reason—the guards would not come near the bedbugs.

Right up until her death in the camp, Corrie's sister, Betsie, was full of praise, encouragement and, most of all, a ceaseless faith in the goodness and power of God. Corrie found it difficult to praise and trust God like her sister, but eventually her heart softened. Like her sister, Corrie discovered the stubborn love of God in the midst of the hell of the concentration camp.

Not long after being released Corrie began to travel and speak about God's love and faithfulness to her in the camp. It was a very different story than most were telling coming out of the horrors of World War II. Like any survivor of the worst life has to offer, Corrie had every human right to be bitter. She had gone through a valley deeper than most of us will ever go through. But she chose not to be.

Then one time early in her travels, not too many years after the war, she was greeting people after her lecture. A man approached her and said, "Do you remember me?" When he identified himself, she immediately remembered— he had been one of the crueler prison guards in the concentration camp, responsible for much of the pain inflicted upon Corrie, Betsie and others. He said, "Corrie, I have become a Christian. Would you forgive me?"

Her mind retorted, *You have got to be kidding me. How can I forgive someone who brought so much pain to me and my family?* The struggle to practice what she had been preaching was intense.

But the Holy Spirit prodded her, "Tell him you forgive him."

Corrie thought, *I can't. I have no forgiveness for that man.* Though God was using her to speak on forgiveness and reconciliation, nothing in her wanted to forgive, but she knew she had to obey—even if she did not feel like it.

She almost had to force the words out of her mouth, "I forgive you." As she spoke in obedience, God began to give her genuine forgiveness.

"And kids," she said that day I attended her lecture in Fullerton, "that is the most beautiful thing God has ever done."

HURT FROM OTHERS

Sometimes we end up in valleys through the cruelty or carelessness of others. Not only do tribs happen, but they sometimes happen because someone else did something terribly wrong—a father or mother, a friend, a minister, a husband or wife, a Nazi concentration camp guard. We did not deserve the hurt they inflicted on us; we were innocent, and yet we bear the harsh brunt of their actions. They have, whether intentionally or not, carried us with them into a thorny valley.

I imagine that as you are reading this you can count on your fingers the people you hold responsible for the biggest hurts in your life. Each of us has a running list in our minds of people who betrayed, abandoned, misused or caused us pain, even if we have decided to forgive them.

To this day, no one has impacted my life spiritually, except for my family, as much as Corrie ten Boom. A host of people had hurt her; some might say they even ruined her life. The man she wanted to marry betrayed her. A friend turned her and her family in for doing something humane. A number of guards at the camp humiliated and harmed her. And one guard in particular had deeply wounded her.

As a young girl she had probably imagined that her life would turn out totally different—married to a man who loved her, living in a safe place, experiencing a fulfilling career and having children and grandchildren. She could not have foreseen ending up an elderly, never-married woman who had lost her family to an unspeakably cruel regime. Anyone of lesser stuff would have given up, but Corrie chose to take her life to a higher level, convinced that "God works for the good of those who love him, who have been called according to his purpose" (Rom. 8:28).

How do you forgive that many people who have inflicted such heinous wounds on you? How do you rise above the garbage to attain even higher levels of abundant life in God? To this day I marvel at the grace God gave to Corrie ten Boom. The same grace is available to you today, no matter what obstacles life has tossed your way.

JOSEPH

It is hard enough when you are going through hell because of your own bad choices. If nothing else, you feel that you are simply getting what you deserve. But it can be absolutely infuriating when you did absolutely nothing wrong. Or maybe you were even trying to help people or simply doing the right thing, yet somehow it seems to have backfired and is now being used against you.

This is what happened to Joseph—and more than once. The story of Joseph, and the eleven other sons of Jacob, is told in Genesis chapters 37–50. More recently it was made popular by Andrew Lloyd Webber's *Joseph and the Amazing Technicolor Dreamcoat*. Like a good movie or novel, this true-life adventure is full of murder, betrayal, deceit and, finally, redemption. Joseph is the pivotal character, always the innocent victim who somehow keeps coming out on top.

Like our life's journey, his life's journey between God's call and the realization of his dreams was pitted with valleys.

The action begins when Joseph is asked by his father to check on his brothers who had gone to graze Jacob's flocks near Shechem. Joseph, in obedience, travels to Shechem, but he doesn't find them there. Being told where they might be, he continues on to Dothan. Sure enough, he finds them, but as he is approaching from a distance, his brothers scheme to kill him. That's right, his own flesh and blood hatch a plot to murder him. Talk about a dysfunctional family!

From his end Joseph was trying to do something good for his brothers, even though he knew they did not like him. He had obeyed his father and not given up when at first he didn't find them. He made good decisions and got burned. Almost every valley that Joseph walked through, he walked through because he had done the right thing.

Why did his brothers dislike him? Two reasons. One, he had dreams that on the surface appeared to his family to be arrogant visions of personal grandeur. His family could not see or understand what God was doing through one of their own. Two, while helping his brothers tend the flocks on an earlier occasion, Joseph had brought their father a bad report about them.

I know what it is like to bring a bad report about fellow workers to Dad. My father owned a gas station for twenty-six years, and I worked there off and on as I was growing up. The other employees knew I was his son, but whenever Dad would leave, the quality of work would drop dramatically—even with me still on the premises. I wonder what the work quality was like when I left? Most workers were eye-pleasers, always cleaning things up whenever Dad was around, but typically standing around doing nothing when he left.

I used to come home and give my dad a bad report. "Hey,

Dad, once you drive away, the work goes downhill quick."

Maybe this is what Joseph did with his brothers. I doubt he had any malice. I think he was doing it just to let his dad know how the business was doing—just as I would do with my dad. Nevertheless, as might be expected, this did not make his brothers happy.

On top of all this, the Bible also says Jacob loved Joseph more than his other sons because he had been born to him in his old age. Jacob made him a coat of many colors, which was a sign of honor.

To his brothers, then, Joseph was nothing more than a spoiled brat with delusions of grandeur who liked to tattle. So when Joseph arrived on his father's errand, his brothers threw him into a dry cistern to hold him until they could figure out how to perform the dirty deed. Joseph cried out for help, but his brothers ignored his pleas. In fact, they rather coldly sat down and ate to their hearts' content.

This is not even a crime of passion; it is a chilling account of an innocent young man falling victim to evil men—in this case, his own brothers. As sometimes happens in life, those who should have loved him the most hurt him the most.

KAREN

I know a woman named Karen who, like Joseph, went through an extremely difficult valley a few years ago—one that was created by the cruelty of others. It began when Karen's mother, father and sister were killed one night in their home by an embittered relative. Only because she was not there was Karen's life spared.

Working through her own grief in the face of personal tragedy was just the beginning of the challenges she faced. Immediately Karen took her sister's children in, but soon after, she went through a divorce that devastated her own children. One thing began to pile upon another, and she felt as if her life was falling apart.

Karen made it through what must have seemed like her own personal hell with the help of friends and church family. She refused to quit, choosing instead to keep her eyes on God while taking things one day at a time. In time God provided her with a wonderful new husband.

Amazingly, when Karen talks about the situation, she sticks to themes of love and forgiveness.

"I don't hate the person who killed my parents and sister," she told our church. "I truly pray that he asks God for forgiveness. I know that God can forgive anybody for anything."

One of the questions people ask Karen is where she got the strength to go through such a devastating experience. Her answer is always the same: "If you don't have God, you don't have anything. He has been the one to get me through this. He is going to use this tragedy for His glory. If He wants me to impact the town of Covina or just my family, it doesn't matter. I am ready to go. I am ready to do what He wants me to do."

Forgiving is one of the most difficult things a person can do. The heart resists like a stubborn pack mule; the mind reels at the possibility that the person who hurt you won't get justice. But Jesus said in Matthew 10:8, "Freely you have received, freely give." It is central to the gospel, like it or not. And yet there is much misunderstanding about it, too. Try answering the questions in the following quiz.

1. True or false—A person should not be forgiven until he or she asks for forgiveness.

2. True or false—Forgiveness includes minimizing the offense and the pain caused by that offense.

3. True or false—Forgiveness includes restoring trust and reuniting relationships.

4. True or false—You have really not forgiven until you have forgotten the offense.

5. True or false—When I see someone else get hurt, it is my Christian duty to forgive the offender.

A careful reading of the Gospels shows us that, perhaps surprisingly, the answer to all of these questions is false.

FORGIVENESS IS NOT CONDITIONAL

This means that forgiveness cannot be earned, bought or bargained for. There is an old movie, *The End,* starring Burt Reynolds and Dom Deluise. Burt Reynolds' character is informed by the doctors that he is dying. Rather than having to go through the pain of the slow, dying process, he decides to kill himself. The movie is full of the comic antics he and his sidekick go through, bumbling one suicide attempt after another—never, of course, succeeding.

In the final suicide attempt at the end of the movie, he decides he is going to kill himself by drowning, so he jumps into the ocean. The plan this time is to swim so far away from the shore that he can never make it back alive. As he approaches the point of no return, Dom Deluise dashes on the beach, yelling at his struggling friend in the water, "The doctor's report was wrong. The office inadvertently mixed up your test results with somebody else's. You are not dying. You are healthy."

At first Burt Reynolds cannot hear what his friend is shouting, but as soon as he figures it out, he knows he is in trouble. He is dangerously far from the shore; he may not make it back. Though I forget the specifics of the dialogue, I remember that he starts making bargains with God: "God, if you help me make it back, 75 percent of what I earn is going to go to You for the rest of my life. I will live on 25 percent. And I'll go to church every Sunday." As he gets closer to shore, making survival increasingly seem like a real possibility, he keeps changing the deal. "That's right, God—like I said—60 percent. It's Yours. I'll be in church most Sundays." The closer to shore he gets, the smaller his commitment to God becomes, "45 percent—30 percent—10 percent." By the time he is standing on the sand, he says, "If I have time, maybe I will go to church once in a while." Then he walks on the shore.

It is a funny scene because it is so typical. When in trouble, or in the middle of a valley we don't think we will survive, we bargain with God. "God, if You just heal me of this, I promise I will never cuss again." Or, "God, if You bring my spouse back, I promise I'll never speak harshly to him (or her) ever again." Such promises, though sincere at the time, are seldom, if ever, kept. But there is something in our human nature that insists on paying for what we receive. If God is to help us, we reason, then we must have something to offer Him.

It goes against our nature to receive help from God with no strings attached. It is wonderful, but difficult to accept. It is even more difficult, however, to offer that same kind of unconditional forgiveness to others. Yet this is exactly what a forgiving God asks of His children. Paul says it very simply in Colossians 3:13: "Bear with each other and forgive whatever grievances you may have against one another. Forgive as the Lord forgave you." Sometimes I wonder which of the two is more difficult—freely receiving forgiveness for my own sins, or forgiving others who have treated me with no respect or consideration.

If learning to receive forgiveness from the Lord is a key to making it through the valley of our own mistakes, then learning to forgive others is the key to making it through the valley others have caused. This can be difficult. For example, sometimes people blast you when they come to you asking for your forgiveness. As a pastor, this happens to me all too often. Typically, a well-intentioned person ever so dramatically says to me, "Pastor, I have to ask you for your forgiveness." They proceed to make reference to a situation I don't even remember. Then, as they ask me to forgive them, they insult me by telling me something I did wrong that hurt them. "One time when you were preaching, you said such-and-such, and that really hurt me, and I have hated you for so long. But now God has dealt with me and I would like you to forgive me for hating you." I know such apologies are usually sincere and the person is trying to be spiritual, but somehow their asking for forgiveness ends up being focused on what I did wrong!

Forgiveness needs to be unconditional, with no strings attached, whether we are on the receiving or the giving end. And remember, there is a difference between being wrong and being wounded. A wrong is not a wound. When we are wronged or when we wrong, forgiveness needs to take place. But a lot of things hurt us that are not necessarily wrong, and they do not require forgiveness. Sometimes we just have to learn to accept each other, even if we chafe at each other's differences.

FORGIVENESS DOES NOT MINIMIZE THE HURT, PAIN OR SERIOUSNESS OF THE OFFENSE

We all have a natural tendency when someone apologizes to say, "Ah, don't worry about it. It was no big deal." That may or may not be true, but for the person doing the apologizing it could be a very big deal—just apologizing may be traumatic. Remember Fonzie from the television show *Happy Days* trying to say "Sorry"? Giving and receiving forgiveness, even over small issues, is a godlike quality not to be taken lightly.

Forgiveness may be unconditional, but it does not minimize the pain, the hurt and the seriousness of the offense. Just because you give forgiveness to someone or receive forgiveness yourself, it does not mean that it no longer hurts. A husband may be sitting next to his wife, who years ago forgave him for that affair, but the genuine forgiveness does not make the seriousness, the pain or the hurt of what the affair did to her and the children any less.

FORGIVENESS IS NOT RESUMING A RELATIONSHIP WITHOUT CHANGE

Forgiveness and reconciliation are two different things. Forgiveness is unconditional. Reconciliation is conditional. This is a huge point that most Christians miss. Forgiveness does not necessarily have to end in reconciliation. If you have lived with a physically abusive husband, you ought to forgive that husband if you are a Christian woman. But that does not mean that now you will stay with him or go back to him without major changes taking place.

You may have drug-addicted kids who come home and say, "I got saved. God forgave me. Do you forgive me, Mom and Dad?"

"We forgive you."

"Great! Can I take the car and have some money?"

"No."

Why? Because forgiveness, while beautiful, does not make everything all better instantly. It is not an easy way out of problems. It is not a shortcut to or a replacement for change. And it does not mean that a relationship ought to be resumed without some serious changes taking place. Along with forgiveness, you need three things to reconcile.

Change

This is what repentance is really all about. *Repentance* was the first word of the Old Testament prophets, of John the Baptist and of Jesus. *To repent* literally means "to change your mind." If you want to reconcile, and you are abusing your wife, you will have to change before reconciliation can take place. "But she forgave me." Yes, that was the first step, but if you want her to live with you, you have to show a pattern of new behavior. You have to be willing to repent.

Restitution

Most people do not even know what this word means anymore. *Restitution* means that you make your best effort, as far as is appropriate, to make amends to the people that you have harmed. If you are a bank robber who comes to church and gets saved, you are instantly forgiven, but you have robbed people and, quite frankly, ought to do your best to make restitution to those you have hurt. Zaccheus paid back four times the amount he had cheated from people after Jesus got hold of his heart. This teaching can be taken overboard and turned legalistic, but the core idea of restitution is very important; it ought to flow naturally from a repentant heart.

Rebuilding trust

Forgiveness is unconditional. Trust has to be earned. We can truly forgive someone, an addicted child or wayward husband, without extending to them unwarranted trust. In fact, that is how it should be. Forgiveness happens instantly, but rebuilding trust takes time. Suppose, for example, an apparently happily married woman decides to leave her husband and children in an effort to "discover herself." In so doing, she makes a huge withdrawal from the trust bank. In one fell swoop she wipes out the family. Later, like the prodigal son, she decides to come home. Forgiveness may or may not be offered, but the restored trust of her husband and children is not so quickly or easily gained. Deposits of consistent change and perhaps some needed restitution must be made. The kids may still love their mom, but it does not follow that they will automatically trust her simply because her conscience eventually caught up with her. Who could blame them?

Forgiveness is instantaneous. Trust must be rebuilt. Forgiveness lets the person off the hook, but trust takes a careful look before being offered. We are obligated to forgive, but we are not obligated to stupidly trust.

FORGIVENESS IS NOT FORGETTING WHAT HAPPENED

Most of us have heard of the famous feud between the Hatfields and McCoys, two real families who fought so bitterly after the Civil War that their story became almost legendary. Recently, in the state of Kentucky, hundreds of members of both families held a mass picnic and played five innings of softball as a light-hearted act to say that the feud was finally over.[1]

Obviously, those families will never forget that they inherited such a famous rivalry, but they were able to put it behind them, even making light of what had been a not-so-funny history.

The Bible tells us that God not only forgives our sins, but He also forgets them. He buries them in the depths of the ocean and posts a no fishing sign. He remembers our sins no more.

But we are not God, and we err when we think that to forgive someone we have to forget the offense. It is physically impossible for human beings to do that, aside from having some kind of head trauma or brain damage. If you are waiting to forget in order to forgive, you are going to be waiting forever.

The greater the pain, the more we remember the offense. The hurt may fade with time, but it never really goes away. Many counselors and even a few preachers are pretty skilled in bringing people to tears as they reopen the wounds of the past. The key to healing, however, is not found in trying to forget our past or in a superficial "inner healing." I am all for authentic inner healing, which brings the healing touch of Jesus to hurts that have never really healed, but I am not for manipulating people's emotions by prying open their wounds.

God offers something better than forgetting. That is remembering without the pain. It may take a while to get to the place where we can recall the situation without feeling the accompanying pain. Nevertheless, the healing will come. An emotional scar or two may remain, but the tenderness is gone.

Not all scars are bad. They can remind us of the healing grace of God over an area that was once tender. A scar can serve as personal proof that Romans 8:28 is true—"God works for the good of those who love him, who have been called according to his purpose." You will remember what you went through, but be able to say, "I met Jesus there." In the fiery furnace of your past hurts, you will see not only Shadrach, Meshach and Abednego, but a fourth man standing right there with you—One who looks like the Son of Man.

FORGIVENESS IS NOT YOUR INALIENABLE RIGHT WHEN YOU WERE NOT THE ONE HURT

Contrary to popular opinion, we do not have the right to throw around forgiveness to people when we were not the victims. In America right now you are looked at as strange if you do not forgive everyone on the spot, even when they did not harm you. After one of the recent school shootings I watched the news and saw that someone had hung a sign in the hallway that said, "We forgive you." On the surface this looks like a gracious gesture, and I am sure that the people who put that up were well intentioned. Quite frankly, however, it was not their offense to forgive, at least not primarily. That right really belonged to the families of the victims.

So the cavalier attitude of "forgive and forget," or as they say in New York, "forget about it," is not what is needed to bounce back from life's hurts, scrapes and bruises. Only God can forget, and only the victims of the hurt have the primary right to forgive. I am not the one in position to forgive Hitler for what he did to the Jews, even though my wife is half Jewish. I can never rightfully say, "Adolf, I forgive you." The ones who have the right to say it are the ones who were the victims of Nazi terror, or their families. We cannot offer forgiveness when we are not the one who was offended.

PRACTICAL STEPS

How do you forgive someone who has led you into a deep valley? How do you keep anger, resentment and bitterness from making that valley even deeper and longer? Here are a few things you can do to forgive effectively and move away from bitterness.

Remember how much God has forgiven you.
It is easier to forgive others when you remember where you came from. Some Christians forget. They act as if God found them in the rose garden, not on the trash heap. If you forget where you came from, you tend to minimize God's grace in your life. Jesus said it like this, "Therefore, I tell you, her many sins have been forgiven—for she loved much. But he who has been forgiven little loves little" (Luke 7:47). How much have you been forgiven?

Let God deal with your enemies.

You must give up your right to get even and let God deal with your enemies. If you are set on revenge, you may win a few battles, or you may lose a few, but God will certainly not fight for you. If you pick up the sword, He will sit back and watch. But if you lay down the sword, He will actively pursue justice on your behalf.

Joseph did not spend his life plotting revenge on his brothers. Rather, he prospered wherever God put him. Would you rather your enemies fell into your hands, or God's?

I remember watching a movie when I was a boy in which a crazy preacher went around shooting people and saying, "'Vengeance is mine, I will repay', saith the Lord." Religious fanatics often kill people, if not literally, then with unforgiveness. But that is not the Bible's prescription for our enemies.

Psalm 24:8 declares:

> Who is this King of glory?
>> The LORD strong and mighty,
>> the LORD mighty in battle.

I don't care how good you are in battle; you are not as good as God. Paul says in Romans 12:19, "Do not take revenge, my friends, but leave room for God's wrath, for it is written: 'It is mine to avenge; I will repay,' says the Lord." Forgiveness means giving up your right to get even.

Let God heal your hurts.

Psalm 23:5 notes of God, "You prepare a table before me in the presence of my enemies." The Lord, in the midst of a valley, will give you a break from the action. You may still be going through major turmoil, but now and again He will call a time-out, motion you to the sidelines and say, "Sit out a few plays." Even with enemies, problems and challenges breathing down your neck, God will give you rest and relaxation. He will make you lie down in green pastures and lead you beside still waters.

Those times are precious. You are not yet through the valley, but you still get fed; you let your guard down, and you laugh. For a little while you forget about those who have harmed you. God knows we are only human and can only handle so much, so He provides times of relief and refreshment.

Psalm 23:5 also says, "You anoint my head with oil." Shepherds anoint their sheep with oil to take care of the fly problem. Flies can be more deadly to sheep than wolves. For example, if sheep are not sheared and if their tails are not removed, flies will plant larvae in their wool and skin, and the resulting infection can kill them.

Flies also buzz around sheep's eyes, causing major irritation. But if a sheep's head is doused in oil, it hinders the flies from landing on it. I have been told that sheep that are not properly cared for can resort to banging their heads against a wall in an attempt to bring relief. Sheep, of course, do not have fingers to scratch their faces or shoo away the flies.

I have seen too many Christians attempt to escape the pain of the past without the anointing of the Shepherd. Such efforts end up being just as silly and useless as sheep banging their heads against a wall. We all want to get rid of the pain, but sometimes we just do not know how to do so. If Jesus is our Good Shepherd, and He is, then the smart thing is to stop beating our heads against the wall with all our "home remedies" and allow Him to apply the healing salve of the Holy Spirit.

Sometimes our past hurts just plain old stink! Oil not only has healing properties, but it also comes with a sweet-smelling aroma. I don't know about you, but I do not mind wearing a little of God's aftershave or perfume while I am in the process of having Him clean up my mess. "Pleasing is the fragrance of your perfumes; your name is like perfume poured out" (Song of Sol. 1:3).

The anointing of oil was also used to inaugurate the rule of a new king. Even while we are still in the valley, God wants us to be overcoming, devil-defeating, reigning children of God.

Let God satisfy all your needs.

Psalm 23:5 closes with the words, "My cup overflows." That is a simple way of saying, "God is enough." One major reason many of us get hurt in life is that we expect others to meet needs that only God can meet. We are destined for disappointment in our marriages, our parenting and our relationships with our parents and friends if we expect others to provide for us in ways that only God can.

No person can give you absolute security in life.

No person can give you all the love you need.

No person can make you completely happy.

No person, that is, except God. The only thing that can result from looking to others to meet our needs of security, love and happiness is frustration. God has given us needs that were designed by God to be met by Him and Him alone. It is His way of driving us to Him. I am not saying that others cannot make you happy, give you love or bring you security. But the source of these is God. If you rely on Him, you will never lack.

God will fill your cup to overflowing. I have read that, in ancient times, if the host refilled your cup, it was a sign you were invited to stay longer. If not, time to go. These days, at least where I live, there is no clear signal we give that a guest should leave. Sometimes I go to people's homes, and from the minute I walk in the door I am wondering how long I should stay and at what precise moment I should leave. It's a terrible feeling to overstay your welcome, but it is even worse when guests overstay theirs!

In Bible times they took care of this problem with an unspoken ritual. You knew how long you should stay by how many times the host would fill your cup. Some people were one-cup guests. Others were three-cup guests. According to custom, if the host really liked you and wanted you to stay a long time, he would fill your cup to overflowing, meaning there was more than enough to go around.

God loves you so much that even when you are going through the valley He fills your cup to overflowing. He invites you to stay near Him. He wants to be with you. He is overflowing with love for you.

Listen to the right people.

There is a precious man in our church who is a very talented musician, a terrific father and a faithful husband. He just completed his Ph.D. from a major university in Southern California. He has beaten the odds, for he was born a minority in the ghettos of Los Angeles. When he was young, his father often told him that he was trash and would never amount to anything. For a while, those crushing words, not to mention the prejudices of society, drove him off course, and he became yet another troubled young person on the mean streets of L.A. As a teenager, he punched a teacher and was nearly expelled from school.

Against all odds, his mother told him a different story. She would say, "You are so smart. You can be anything you want. The Bible says you can do all things through Christ who strengthens you." He had to decide whom he was going to listen to—the doom-and-gloom declarations of society and even his own father, or the promises of God as delivered through his mother. Thankfully, he made up his mind to believe his mother, and he has been unstoppable ever since.

When we find ourselves in a valley not of our own choosing, many voices will be quick to offer advice. Some, like Job's well-meaning but misdirected friends, will tell us there is no hope. We might as well curse God and die. But we have a choice of whom we are going to listen to, and that choice will determine if and when we make it out of the valley. Even when there seems to be no hope, there is always God.

Repay evil with good.
I know that sounds syrupy sweet. It is often the last thing we want to hear when we are going through a rough time, especially one that was caused by the person we are supposed to love. Still, we cannot ignore the words of our Lord in Luke 6:27: "I tell you who hear me: Love your enemies, do good to those who hate you, bless those who curse you, pray for those who mistreat you."

Abraham Lincoln was asked one time during a campaign why he was treating his opponent so kindly. "Don't you know," the question probably went, "that you have to destroy your enemies if you want to win the election?"

Lincoln answered the question with a question, "Do I not destroy my enemies when I make them my friends?" Loving your enemies and doing good to those who harm you is not for the weak or fainthearted; it is, however, a principle for winners.

Doing good to those who have hurt us does not mean they have "gotten away" with anything. It does not mean God lets sin slide. Anyone who is counting on that will be in for a big surprise. I would not want to be on the side of those who suppose they can hurt, abuse and sin—all the while trusting the grace of God to forgive them when it is convenient. For example, I have talked to men, seemingly pillars of the community, who have taken me out to lunch and said, "Pastor, I have been coming to the church for a while, and I know that you are acquainted with my wife and kids. I really do have a great family, but the truth is that I have fallen in love with this younger woman at the office. I'm not proud of this, and I never really intended for this to happen or to hurt anybody, but she is so beautiful. I feel so alive again, Pastor. For the first time in years, I feel young again. I actually want to wake up in the morning. I have a purpose for living."

Sometimes they get really emotional: "Oh Pastor, I know it is not right, but to be honest with you, Pastor, I am going to leave my wife and family. Even though it is not right, I think God understands. Don't you think so, Pastor? I believe God will forgive me. Pastor, God is going to forgive me, right?"

About that time I am sorry that I ordered any food. People like that are not looking for forgiveness. They are looking for their actions to be condoned. They want me to say, "It's OK." And indeed, in today's culture it is OK. Sadly, even in much of the church world it has become so common that it seems to be no big deal. You can divorce the spouse that you married in this church, find a new spouse in another church and leave both your churches and find yet another church and start off fresh in life and ministry again. Most churches are perfectly happy to welcome you, either not knowing or not caring about all the garbage of your past.

I am a strong believer in grace, forgiveness and the redeeming power of God, no matter how much we have messed up our lives. God's grace, however, is not cheap. As someone once said of His love—it is not "sloppy agape." Three separate Bible writers pronounce the same thing, "God opposes the proud but gives grace to the humble." (See Proverbs 3:34; James 4:6; 1 Peter 5:5.) Human pride looks to do what it wants without judgment. It looks for ambiguities in the law that will excuse its actions. Humility, on the other hand, is not looking for loopholes. In the end, God will deal justly with all of us.

Develop a lifestyle of forgiveness.

Peter one day was flexing his spiritual muscles in front of Jesus. The Jewish rabbis of that day taught that you could forgive someone up to three times in one day. Peter doubled it and added one for good measure. "Lord, how many times shall I forgive my brother when he sins against me? Up to seven times?" Jesus, not overly impressed, replied, "I tell you, not seven times, but seventy-seven times." Or, as the King James Version says it, "seventy times seven" (Matt. 18:21–22). Whether seventy-seven or seventy times seven, the point is to forgive as often as is necessary.

I have known a few Christians to do the math—seventy times seven, which is four hundred ninety—and claim to be in such a hurtful relationship or situation that they have already met that demand. That is a lot of forgiving in one day, and besides, it misses the point. Jesus is not saying, "Look, if someone fills this new more generous quota, then you are free to do what you want—bless them with a brick."

Forgiveness is a healthy way to live. It is the only alternative to bitterness. Studies have shown that bitterness is one of the most harmful emotions humans can have. It destroys a person like a cancer. Bitterness can and does, in fact, lead to literal physical illnesses that can be deadly. Additionally, hanging on to hurt does nothing to the person who harmed you—it is wasted energy.

If you do not release the person who hurt you, you may even begin to resemble that person. Some of us have become the very thing we hated the most. "I will never be like my father. I will never talk like that or act like that to my children." Now as parents we find ourselves doing just that, often because of hurt, bitterness and unforgiveness. God commands us to live in forgiveness, not because He is trying to make things difficult, but because He wants us to be healthy.

THEY THAT WAIT

A typical response when plodding through a valley of hurt is, "But I don't feel like forgiving! They were the ones who wronged me. They should come to me and apologize first." This may sound good and make sense to our concept of justice, but it only serves to make the valley deeper and longer. If you wait for a change of feelings to forgive, you may wait a lifetime. One of the most important truths I have learned in my lifetime is this—*it is easier to act your way into a feeling than to feel your way into an action.*

I picked up this gem from the recovery movement. For those trying to stay sober and clean, with all their hurts and past failures, this statement is not simply a nice little suggestion; it is a lifeline for health. No one would stay sober or clean if they depended upon how they felt each day. Letting go of pain, regrets and shame is a necessary choice to be made daily—regardless of feelings.

Like me, you may not be a recovering alcoholic or drug addict, but all of us need to forgive when we do not feel like it. Do not wait until you feel like it to forgive. So I say it again—*it is easier to act your way into a feeling than to feel your way into an action.*

Instead of waiting to forgive, forgive now and wait for God to change you. The Book of Isaiah offers wonderful promises for those times when we seem to be carrying more than our share of burdens. For the first thirty-nine chapters Isaiah's prophecies have been primarily those of judgment with no sign of hope. Suddenly, in Isaiah 40, the mood shifts, and the prophet declares:

> Comfort, comfort my people, says your God. Speak tenderly to Jerusalem, and proclaim to her that her hard service has been completed, that her sin has been paid

for, that she has received from the LORD's hand double for all her sins.

—ISAIAH 40:1–2

Then, a few verses later, comes one of my favorite verses in the Bible, Isaiah 40:31.

But they that wait upon the LORD shall renew their strength; they shall mount up with wings as eagles; they shall run, and not be weary; and they shall walk, and not faint.

—KJV

God has not forgotten you in the valley. He sees your hurt and pain. And just like in the Book of Isaiah, help will suddenly come your way. Only do not wait to forgive, and do wait upon the Lord.

I must confess that patience has never been one of my virtues. I grew up before the advent of Nintendo and Sega Genesis. Back in my time we used to get a big thrill over something called a kite. My dad and I would make one from scratch. We had to cut up cloth to make a tail, attach the string and so on.

Whenever my dad and I worked together on making the kite, I always was impatient. I wanted to get right out and fly it. Without exception, it seemed that on the day I finished my kite there was no wind, so I would take the kite out in the yard and run hard. The kite would go up as long as I ran, but the moment I stopped it would head back down. I would want it to fly so bad that I would try again and again, running back and forth.

That is the perfect picture of some Christian lives. As long as you feel that you are really working at it, you can get a little bit off the ground. Maybe you are not soaring like your spiritual heroes, but if you try hard, you can keep it going.

But we all grow weary. Paul grew weary. Joseph grew weary. Even Jesus grew weary. Problems can pile on, but when they do, God will send you a breeze to lift you high. You will not have to toil any longer. You will mount up with wings as eagles. You will run and not grow weary, and you will walk and not faint. That is the promise God has for you.

It's true: You can never expect too little from people. The moment you think they can't do any worse, they will.

But you can never expect too much from God. And with Him in charge, you can walk through the valley of unfair hurts knowing He will take care of you.

Chapter 4

Valleys of Sovereignty

I was standing in the sound booth of Faith Community Church before the Sunday evening service when a woman ran up to me, visibly shaken.

"Pastor," she said. "Something terrible has happened. Danny has been run over by a car."

Immediately I dismissed the thought as fiction, thinking she surely must be mistaken. How could such a thing happen? He was just a small boy. I couldn't believe the information I was hearing, and so I called the hospital to confirm that it was Danny. The hospital would confirm no details, only that he was indeed there, so I left the service in the hands of my staff and the visiting evangelist.

I had watched Michael and Helene, Danny's parents, grow up from their young teens. Helene was a friend of our family, and Michael had been in my youth group. I had performed their wedding ceremony. Michael had even served on staff when I launched a church in West Covina, where I pastor today. Helene had been my secretary. Later, we sent them out to plant a church. They were friends, almost family.

The moment I walked into the hospital I was met by a

doctor and a policeman. They pulled me aside and explained the gravity of the situation. I could scarcely believe what I was hearing. Not only had Danny been run over, but he had accidentally been run over by Michael as he was leaving for church that night. Danny had been at the next door neighbor's house, and seeing his dad through the window, he had come running across the yard and driveway to say good-bye to his daddy at precisely the wrong time.

"Danny will not live," the doctor told me. "You need to go minister to them."

There is nothing more heartbreaking than having to step into a situation where parents may be losing a child. I had never faced a situation where one of the parents, good people, had inadvertently been involved in the tragedy. When I walked into the waiting room, people were already with the panicked parents, praying and believing for God to spare the child's life. I joined them, praying in faith, knowing that doctors are sometimes wrong and that God could over-turn any medical diagnosis.

We prayed fervently.

Our hearts ached together.

We cried and shouted and believed God to perform a miracle.

We interceded as best we knew how.

And a few hours later, Danny died.

Michael and Helene were crushed. All of us were deflated and emotionally exhausted. Not knowing what else to do, I went home with one word ringing in my mind: *Why?*

THE SOVEREIGNTY FACTOR

We enter some valleys that are the result not of our own sin nor of the sin of others. They are the valleys we go through for no clear reason and no apparent purpose. We can find no one to blame, search as we might for answers as to why we are in such a forsaken place. These are perhaps the hardest valleys of all because they call into question the very character of God.

Whom do we blame for hurts that seem to come out of thin air? God? The devil? Fate? Ourselves?

How do we explain the young mother who gets cancer and dies, leaving four children?

On a larger scale, how do we explain the cycle of famine and war in Africa and elsewhere in the world?

How do we explain the prevalence of ravaging diseases in the world?

These questions take on added significance when we boldly preach and firmly believe in the goodness, grace and healing power of a loving God. Is there something we have done wrong, or something vital left undone?

There is a couple in our church whose teenage son was at a church service on a Wednesday night. On the way home, he stopped at an ATM because he had given his last ten dollars in the offering. He was brutally shot and killed by a thief while getting his money out.

Another couple I know recently lost a son while on an excursion to the mountains when he drowned in a lake.

I read in the newspaper about a thirty-one-year-old man who was awaiting a kidney transplant. Word arrived that a match had been found, and the family was overjoyed. They took the man into surgery, but when doctors opened the organ shipment container, they found a heart. Someone had mislabeled the boxes. The man died a month later, still waiting for a new kidney. Officials from the organ bank called it "a very unfortunate human error."[1]

We all have stories like this to tell. We watch sad stories unfold almost daily on the news, hoping that nothing like that ever comes near us. They stick like burrs in our spirits. How could God let that happen? What good could come from it?

The most common question any pastor will have to answer is, "Why does God allow suffering and evil?" Or put in an even more troubling manner, "Why do bad things happen to good people?" It is perhaps the predominant question in both philosophy and religion, and it can be personalized in a million ways.

- "Why does God allow my Christian grandmother to suffer through Alzheimer's disease?"
- "Why did my dad die in a car wreck when I was just a girl?"
- "Why did God allow my brother to be molested as a child?"

Some Christians are forced to deal with this question early on when a parent dies, and adults, in their rush to console, say things like, "Your mommy is in heaven with Jesus. She is happier now than she ever has been. God must have needed your mommy." Even a child has the ability to think, *Yeah, right! God needed my mommy more than I do, and He just took her. Well, I'm having nothing to do with a God like that.*

Many great thinkers have wrestled with this issue, and frankly, they haven't gotten very far. The existence of evil has kept many people from becoming followers of Christ, including some of the world's well-known philosophers. Such thinkers reason that the fact that there is such evil and suffering in the world is proof in and of itself that there is no god, and certainly not the God of the Bible.

Edward John Carnell, a brilliant Christian apologist, spelled out the dilemma. "Either God wants to prevent evil, and He cannot do it; or He can do it and does not want to; or He neither wishes to nor can do it; or He wishes to and can do it. If He has the desire without the power, He is impotent; if He can, but has not the desire, He has a malice which we cannot attribute to Him; if He has neither the power nor the desire, He is both impotent and evil and consequently not God; if He has the desire and the power, whence comes evil, or why does He not prevent it?"[2]

If the question were merely theological or philosophical, we could reduce it to theoretical debate or even ignore it, but we don't have that convenience. Evil surrounds us—just read the city section of your local newspaper. The consequences are staggering, causing many otherwise good people to turn their backs on God, saying, "I will not and cannot serve a God who allows evil and undeserved pain and suffering."

WHICH PATH?

Let's say you are in a deep valley whose cause and purpose you do not understand. You were serving God when this calamity came upon you, and you have served Him ever since, though in great anguish of heart.

Your mind turns time and again to the possible reasons for what is happening. This evil seems personally tailored to hurt you in your most vulnerable places. You wonder how God could love you and stand to see you in such pain. You want the valley to make sense; you want your circumstances to give you some clue into the divine logic that sends joy and tragedy upon people in a way that appears capricious and random.

Anyone who has been through serious suffering is forced to reach some conclusions about God. How we respond to personal tragedy will dictate how we relate to God, whether we have fellowship with Him or whether we will carry bitterness toward Him.

"We don't know if God is there or not."

Philosophers like Bertrand Russell argue that agnosticism is the best option. Russell declared, "I'm not contending in a dogmatic way that there is not a God. What I'm contending is that we don't know that there is."[3]

Agnostics try to walk a tightrope between faith and unbelief, asserting that human beings simply do not have enough information to decide whether or not God even exists, much less know anything about Him. We simply do not have enough knowledge to know for sure whether God is behind our tragedy, or whether He is to be trusted or believed in at all. Many agnostics are confident that if they are indeed wrong and find themselves standing before God in judgment, they would have a legitimate case to plead ignorance. For agnostics, no just God could ever send anyone to hell or a place of reckoning based on the vastly insufficient evidence offered to human beings.

"There is no God."

We can take the view of the atheist, who says emphatically that God does not exist. People like the French philosopher Albert Camus and filmmaker Woody Allen hold this view: Life frequently is absurd, even downright stupid. There are no answers. We might laugh, we might cry, but ultimately there is no reason why. The best anyone can do is create some meaning out of the chaos of human existence by making choices that hopefully will bring some personal fulfillment and meaning. Life as a whole, nevertheless, remains a cosmic accident with no purpose or meaning.

"Whatever happens is God's will."

On the other side, religious people around the world have reached the opposite conclusion about suffering. Muslims believe that anything and everything that happens is God's will. The answer to pain and suffering, then, is to passively submit to the will of Allah. Though we may not understand why, all suffering and pain have a divine, if sometimes hidden, purpose.

Surprisingly, some Christians and Jews believe practically the same thing. They lean heavily on the idea of predestination, which states that nothing happens by chance or accident. The ways of God are inscrutable and unknowable, His will mysterious. Pain and suffering are to be endured as good soldiers, for ours is not to reason why; ours is but to do and die. The future cannot be changed; it is a *fait accompli*. When taken to an extreme, this view breeds a *"que sera, sera"* attitude, which can breed a flippant acceptance of whatever life throws our way, good and bad.

While there is an element of truth in this viewpoint, I do not believe that everything that happens on Planet Earth is what God wants. At the risk of oversimplification, God's will can be divided into two categories: His purpose and His desire. God's purposes cannot be thwarted, no matter what happens. For example, Jesus Christ is going to come again, no matter what you or I do, no matter what any nation does, no matter how the planet gets polluted, no matter how many wars there are. That is the unchangeable purpose of God. On the other hand, God's clear desire is for all to be saved. Peter says, "He is patient with you, not wanting anyone to perish, but everyone to come to repentance" (2 Pet. 3:9). Despite God's desire, will all in fact be saved? The sad answer is no.

"My suffering is my fault."

There is yet another view we can adopt when walking through this valley. That view says that any suffering we go through is due to a defect in our own spiritual character or not understanding the promises of God. People of this persuasion often quote Jesus in John 10:10: "I am come that they might have life, and that they might have it more abundantly" (KJV). Anything less than a joyful, pain-free life is viewed as falling short of God's best.

According to some, it is never God's will for anyone to live less than sixty or seventy years; never for them to be less than prosperous financially; never for them to come down with a terminal disease; never for any personal tragedy to befall them. If something awful does happen, it is more than likely due to a lack of faith, because God is perfect, and our problems cannot be His will. If your mom died when you were a child, the problem was on the human end. As sure as God wants everyone to be saved, He wants everyone to be healed, so something somewhere was blocking His best. Somewhere, in every human pain, there is a lack of faith that has stunted God's perfect plan.

Is there truth to this? Absolutely. Lack of faith and disobedience can clearly hinder the miracle-working power of God. The Bible says that Jesus Himself could do no miracles in His hometown of Nazareth due to their unbelief. (See Mark 6:4–5.) What God wants to do for us is often blocked or limited by our lack of faith, or perhaps our unconfessed sin, our pride or the ill treatment of our spouse.

Still, not every valley can be explained away so neatly and easily. It would be wrong to go up to hurting people and say, "Well, dear, if you just had more faith you would not be in this mess." Jesus was moved to heal by faith, but He always had a sense of compassion about Him. I would be furious with anyone who flippantly told a suffering member of my congregation that they wouldn't be sick or suffering if only they had stronger faith. Apart from the lack of compassion some demonstrate, that might not even be the case. People of great faith, humility and understanding of the Word do indeed go through times of suffering. (See Isaiah 53:3; James 5:10–11; 1 Peter 2:19–21.)

"What goes around comes around."
Eastern religions and philosophy are becoming increasingly

popular in the West. The result has been a growing belief in karma, which teaches that every bad thing that happens to you happens in response to something bad that you did—if not in this life, then in a previous one. The "yin and yang" supposedly balance things out. If you suffer more than most other people in this life, it is thought that you must have done something in a previous life to deserve it.

While this idea may be attractive because of its round-about justice and because it gives a simple explanation for suffering and misery, there is nothing biblical about it. Karma is not simply a philosophy of life, but a religious conviction. Belief in karma flows from the concept of reincarnation, a concept that the Bible opposes. Hebrews 9:27 unequivocally states, "And as it is appointed unto men once to die, but after this the judgment" (KJV). Yes, it's a nice idea that what goes around comes around, but I do not believe that we go through valleys because of something we did in a former life.

GOD AND EVIL

God did not create evil. The creation account in Genesis 1 affirms over and over that God looked at what He had made and "saw that it was good." After creating human beings it even goes from good to "very good." The Bible tells us that God is the author of every perfect thing.

When God made humans, He gave to us a unique gift—moral choice. That is, we have the ability to distinguish between good and bad, right and wrong, and to freely choose between the two. The animal world works on basic instinct. No animal, no matter how well trained or seemingly intelligent, has the power to make moral choices. A lion on the Serengeti plains of Africa is never smitten with the pangs of a guilty conscience after killing a baby gazelle. The lion never thinks to itself, "Oh no, maybe I should not have done that! Gazelles deserve to live, too. Maybe that gazelle was a young mother. What have I done?" Monkeys, dogs or other animals can be trained to make choices, but they can never be trained to make moral decisions for themselves. They simply don't have the capacity. God has reserved that for you and me.

Have you ever seen any museums or libraries built by and for dogs? Only human beings have the unique God-given capacity to appreciate a beautiful sunset, create great works of art and author noble pieces of literature. But along with that capacity for good comes the possibility of bad. Wrapped up in genuine freedom is the potential for evil. All evil is, at least indirectly, the result of the abuse of moral freedom.

What about so-called acts of nature that result in tragedy? For example, what about a hurricane that destroys house and home, taking innocent lives? Such "acts of God" are the result of the laws of the physical universe, which operate on the principle of cause and effect. Hurricanes, tornadoes and storms do not, of course, personally target certain individuals for devastation.

Jesus pointed out in Luke that victims of accidents, contrary to the common thinking of His day, had not done anything to deserve their fate. At this time people thought that if you truly lived a righteous life, nothing bad would happen to you. Conversely, if something bad did happen—even what we might call today a random act of nature—they believed it had to be due to something bad, perhaps hidden sin, in the victim's life. Jesus dispelled such erroneous thinking: "Do you think they were more guilty than all the others living in Jerusalem? I tell you, no!" (Luke 13:4–5). Many are innocent victims of the random effects of nature.

Before the Fall of man in the Garden, the physical universe

held no such threats. Sin thus not only affected human beings, but it also did something to nature. Perhaps Paul alludes to this in Romans when he noted that "creation was subjected to frustration" and is looking forward to being "liberated from its bondage to decay" (Rom. 8:20–21). Whatever the case might be, we do know this—when Christ returns we will have no more need to fear even the forces of nature. The entire moral and physical universe will have been subjected to the lordship of Christ. Until then, God can and does protect His children, and even when apparent disaster does strike, He specializes in bringing triumph out of tragedy.

Why did God go ahead and create humanity, knowing that evil would riddle our world—at least for a while? We do not have the complete answer to that question, but we do know that, in His perfect wisdom and love, He knew it was the best way. He knew He could work it all together so that, in the end, He had a perfect universe, full of happiness, with people who had moral freedom and who still chose their Creator. His plan and Person was Jesus Christ, whose mission was to redeem us. His design is to work all things out for the good for those who love Him and are called according to His purpose.

This means that, ultimately, even things that God doesn't want to happen will be woven together for our good—if we allow Him to be the Designer of our lives. Corrie ten Boom would do needlepoint during her lectures. In conclusion she would say, "We see life from the viewpoint that you all see my needlework." And from the underside it did look like a mess—thread and yarn everywhere, stringy and chaotic. Then she would say, "But God looks at life from this direction," and she would turn it over and there would be a beautiful design that she had been working on. The difference was in the perspective. What from one angle might look like an unmitigated mess is from another angle a beautiful design.

The Christian response to evil is, "We don't know why some of these things happen, but some day we will understand. It's inexplicable now, but God will work this out for good because we love Him and are called according to His purpose."

DANNY

Michael and Helene asked me to perform Danny's funeral, but I had no clue what I was going to say. I knew I could easily pick something out of the Bible and make it work, but I did not want to stand up there and give my usual funeral message. I felt I needed a fresh word from the Lord, but God had not shed any light on the situation. The walls of heaven seemed to be closed to me.

Honestly, I was upset and hurting, though certainly not as much as Michael, Helene and their family. The situation had made me angry with God. The night before the funeral I was still frustrated and confused, so I decided to take a walk. It was an unusually clear and beautiful night in Southern California. The more I paced back and forth, the more resentful I became, until finally I said, "God, if You don't give me a word, I will stand up at that pulpit tomorrow and say, 'Folks, I have no clue what to say,' and I will sit down."

I meant it. I was not going to simply go through the motions. Then I began to complain to God. "It isn't fair. Why did this have to happen to them?" I had known Michael and Helene for a long time, and they were sincere believers who had dedicated their lives to serving the Lord. Is this how they were to be repaid?

One sudden and unexpected incident had messed up their whole lives. Sure, there had been many wonderful times with Danny, but from here on they would have to look at the past through tragedy-colored glasses. I remembered when Michael and Helene first met, when they were light and happy young teenagers. They had no idea that life had this in store for them. Now what does the future hold? Oh, sure, time helps, but time never really heals. Such were my thoughts and expressions of frustration to the Lord.

What happened next stands as one of the most significant experiences of my life. I am not prone to visions, but God gave me one that night. I had been looking up at the sky, and suddenly, I saw Jesus' face. He wore this funny expression— the kind a parent gets when a child is throwing a temper tantrum over not getting a cookie, and the parent knows full well there are cookies in the cupboard, but still he watches him throw the tantrum.

That is the kind of look that Jesus gave me, and it made me even angrier. I do not like to be patronized. I felt like a little kid who has cried so hard that when he stops, he has aftershock hiccups. The Lord looked at me and said, "Is that all?"

I said, "Yeah."

Then He repeated to me the essence of what I had said. He said, "So you are mad because something that takes place in a moment can change everything forever?"

I said, "That's right. Why couldn't this have happened to someone else? I would not wish it on my greatest enemy, but if it had to happen to someone, why couldn't it happen to some of the jerks I know? Why did it have to happen to a good couple that were simply trying to do nothing but serve You?"

Intellectually, I knew that millions of people face various misfortunes every day. Michael and Helene were not the first, and they would not be the last. Every three seconds someone dies. That knowledge, however, did absolutely nothing to ease the pain. The Lord said, "You think this moment has messed up everything. You suppose things will never be the same again. But Jim, do you want to see a moment that is going to change all other moments?"

With that, His expression changed and a beautiful smile came on His face. He held up His hand and snapped His fingers, and as it would in a movie, the sky behind Him was rolled away. The heavens parted, and there were countless numbers of angels and saints clothed in white, including Danny. They had the most beautiful expressions on their faces. As sad as Michael and Helene were, that is how happy they all were.

Then the Lord said, "In a moment, in the twinkling of an eye."

That was all He said, but the message was communicated to my heart: Miracles can happen as suddenly as tragedies. And the time will come, perhaps when we least expect it, when in a moment, in the twinkling of an eye, everything will change. And as quickly as those tragic moments changed our lives, we shall be changed forever, when the trumpet sounds and the dead in Christ shall rise, and we shall be caught up to be with the Lord in the air.

I went to the funeral the next day with that fresh word from God. I spoke about miracles. It did not make the pain or the tears any less real, but it reminded us of the hope we have. Paul told the Thessalonians concerning the death of loved ones that although believers cry real tears and feel real hurts, we ought not "to grieve like the rest of men, who have no hope" (1 Thess. 4:13). And I know that even for people who have been through unspeakably difficult valleys, there will come a day when the tears stop flowing, when the sobbing turns to laughter.

Where are Michael and Helene today? Most couples who face a tragedy like this end up getting a divorce. Michael and

Helene trusted God and not the statistics. They are happily married, have two wonderful kids and are pastoring a church in Southern California. Has it been tough? Yes! But God is healing them, and they are able to minister and speak into people's lives—especially those who have gone through terrible tragedies—with power and authority.

What happened to you may not have been good, but your hurts are not wasted. Your valley is not for nothing. God has something in store for you that literally cannot be imagined, and He will use your valley experiences to help others.

Chapter 5

Giants in the Valley

The battle is never ours, but the Lord's. Throughout the
Bible we see Him leading His people into valleys full of
giants—big problems and daunting odds. There really was a
valley in the Promised Land that the Israelites called the
"valley of giants." It was a frightening place because some
giants still lived there, even after Israel took over.

The valley of giants represents a land of tremendous
opportunity and giant-sized blessings, just as our valleys do.
However, if we cower before the problems, we miss the
blessing. "Our mission," as Captain Kirk of *Star Trek* said,
"is to boldly go where no man has gone before." At least,
that needs to be our attitude.

GRASSHOPPER MENTALITY

Twelve spies went into the land of Canaan and came back
not with just a good report, but with an enormous bunch of
grapes that took two men to carry. They said, "The Lord was
right! The land is good, and it flows with milk and honey."
The spies showed the people the fruit. "Look how big those

grapes are—they're huge! The pomegranates? Enormous!" The Israelites enthusiastically responded, "Awesome! Let's go take it!"

But ten of the spies said, "No way! Do you want to know why the fruit there is so large? Because the people that live there are huge."

> We seemed like grasshoppers in our own eyes, and we looked the same to them.
>
> —NUMBERS 13:33

That is what is I call "grasshopper mentality," and it still afflicts many believers today. Have you noticed that other people's problems never seem as challenging as our own? No matter what anyone else is going through, our own problems are the biggest, messiest and most impossible of all. When we talk to other people, we feel brave and confident that, if we were in their shoes, we could slay their giants in a matter of minutes. But when we look at our own problems, our knees quiver. Why is that? Because when we are in the valley of the giants, we tend to lose perspective. Our eyes become fixated on the problems and challenges, and before we know it, we lose sight of just how big our God really is.

Joshua and Caleb chose to keep their eyes on the Lord, looking to the solution rather than the problem. Their perspective was quite different from the perspective of the rest of Israel.

> And do not be afraid of the people of the land, because we will swallow them up. Their protection is gone, but the LORD is with us. Do not be afraid of them.
>
> —NUMBERS 14:9

Numerous times in the Book of Psalms, King David exhorted people to "magnify the LORD with me, and let us exalt his name together" (Ps. 34:3, KJV). Consider that word *magnify.* It means "to enlarge" or "expand." Does focusing on the Lord and praising Him make Him any bigger than He already is? Of course not. God is God whether we praise Him or not. What happens when we praise God is that our perspective changes.

When we focus on our problems, we make them bigger than they really are, and we develop "grasshopper mentality." When we focus on God, our problems shrink and, like Joshua and Caleb, we begin to believe we "can swallow them up."

Even after entering into the Promised Land, serious problems remained for Israel. Perhaps a touch of grasshopper mentality remained. The tribes of Ephraim and Manasseh, for example, were having trouble enjoying their inheritance. "Yet the Manassites were not able to occupy these towns, for the Canaanites were determined to live in that region" (Josh. 17:12).

Some of us have been promised great things in life by God—a great marriage, a great business, a great career, a great ministry—but it has not come to fruition yet because there are enemies that refuse to acknowledge they belong to God. These enemies may be remnants of our past that we should have dealt with long ago, but for some reason we allowed them to linger.

If we cannot defeat our enemies, containment seems to be the next best thing. "However, when the Israelites grew stronger, they subjected the Canaanites to forced labor but did not drive them out completely" (v. 13). That was a mistake. Some of us get to the brink of victory, subdue the enemy and think everything is fine. Instead, we need to defeat and kill the enemy. Compromise is corruption in the land of promise. If you leave one cancer cell, the body remains in danger. If you willfully indulge in any sin habits, you threaten your own God-given promises.

Rather than taking responsibility for their problems, the tribes of Ephraim and Manasseh did what most believers do—complain and blame the leader!

> The people of Joseph said to Joshua, "Why have you given us only one allotment and one portion for an inheritance? We are a numerous people and the LORD has blessed us abundantly."
>
> —JOSHUA 17:14

When in a valley, it is easy to blame someone else, even God, for not giving us enough—a good enough husband, a good enough job, a good enough amount of money, a good enough house.

Joshua, however, would have none of it. He put the responsibility right back on them.

> "If you are so numerous," Joshua answered, "and if the hill country of Ephraim is too small for you, go up into the forest and clear land for yourselves there in the land of the Perizzites and Rephaites."
>
> —JOSHUA 17:15

In other words, go to the valley of the giants and clear land for yourselves.

Sometimes the issue is not that we lack and need more. What we require might be there right under our nose. Still, when the going gets tough in the valley of the giants, it is easier to ask God for a different valley than to clear the valley we already have. There may be nothing wrong with the land God has given us, but we need to get busy and take it for God. We would rather pray for a financial miracle, then walk out to our mailbox and find a check for $100,000 than to have to actually work hard at the job God has provided. It may seem easier to find a new spouse than work with the one we already have. But as a fine elderly Christian woman about to celebrate her fiftieth anniversary told me one time, "Better the devil you know than the devil you don't know." God grows us into our destiny; there are no shortcuts.

Despite Joshua's encouragement, the people were still not convinced.

> The people of Joseph replied, "The hill country is not enough for us, and all the Canaanites who live in the plain have iron chariots, both those in Beth Shan and its settlements and those in the Valley of Jezreel." But Joshua said to the house of Joseph—to Ephraim and Manasseh—"You are numerous and very powerful...though they are strong, you can drive them out."
> —JOSHUA 17:16–18

Joshua had not changed a bit. When he was young he believed God was bigger than the giants, and now that he was an old man, he was more convinced of it than ever. Many of us need to hear his words of wisdom and experience—"You are numerous and very powerful; you can drive them out."

The choice is yours. Like unbelieving Israel, you can magnify your problems, compromise with the enemy and live short of your destiny. Or like Joshua and Caleb, you can magnify the Lord and discover that nothing is too difficult for God.

There was another Israelite who faced a giant in the valley. His name was David, and while the rest of the army ran from Goliath, the nine-foot-tall man who defied God in the valley day after day, David ran straight at him.

His brothers said, "That giant is too big."

David said, "Yeah, too big to miss."

David said to the Philistine, "You come against me with sword and spear and javelin, but I come against you in the name of the LORD Almighty, the God of the armies of Israel, whom you have defied. This day the LORD will hand you over to me, and I'll strike you down and cut off your head. Today I will give the carcasses of the Philistine army to the birds of the air and the beasts of the earth, and the whole world will know that there is a God in Israel. All those gathered here will know that it is not by sword or spear that the LORD saves; for the battle is the LORD's, and He will give all of you into my hands."

—1 SAMUEL 17:45–47

When was the last time you ran toward a giant as David did? When was the last time you looked your biggest problem right in the eye and declared that he would be defeated in the name of the Lord?

David's words were inspiring and his courage contagious. Big problems, however, do not simply run away in fear because we had a momentary blast of courage and spoke the Word with boldness. Goliath was not intimidated one bit. The words had no effect on the Philistine as far as we can tell. If David had not followed them with actions—if he had shouted at Goliath and run away—he would have been no better than the rest of Saul's army. If you feel faith rising up in you to speak to your giants, don't let it end there. The Bible says Goliath charged David, and as soon as you declare war on the giants in your valley, the devil will charge you.

Charge them back! Hit them with a stone. Cut off their heads. No giant has the right to defy God in your life—not the giant of past sin or hurts or wrongs you have suffered. You will surely encounter giants, but the bigger they are, the harder they fall.

TRAPS TO AVOID

No matter what kind of valley we go through, there are practical steps we can take so that we do not succumb to fear and short-circuit God's ultimate plan for us.

Trap #1—Pretend you are not in that valley.

I call this the Clint Eastwood approach. When the going gets tough, be macho, bite the bullet, ignore the hurt and pretend that the valley does not exist. Some people do this in the name of faith, believing that to confess failure, depression or pain is to strengthen the enemy. That is not what the Bible teaches. Every emotion and every experience in life is expressed in the Book of Psalms. High times, low times, times of wanting to die, times of celebration and times of mourning are all expressed by the psalmist. Occasionally David gets angry with God, and at other times he gets so mad at his enemies he tells God to kill them.

Ignoring your pain will never get you through the valley. David confesses in Psalm 39:2–3, "But when I was silent and still, not even saying anything good, my anguish increased. My heart grew hot within me, and as I meditated the fire burned." In other words, when he tried to "tough it out," saying and doing nothing, he just grew more and more angry.

Pretending we are OK when we are not is not faith; it is a recipe for disaster. We need to be honest about what we are going through. If it is a sin area we are dealing with, we need to find a trusted friend or pastor to tell. The apostle James wrote, "Therefore confess your sins to each other and pray for each other so that you may be healed" (James 5:16).

The Clint Eastwood approach also causes us to minimize our valleys. "It's no big deal," we say, and yet we may have been struggling with bitterness for years. Perhaps we have resented someone for a long time for something he (or she) did, and finally he feels convicted and offers an apology. The wrong thing to say is, "No biggie. Don't worry about it." On the surface, such a response may sound humble and even spiritual, but it is neither honest nor healing to the person apologizing. Let him into your heart. Tell her it hurt you, and then honestly forgive. Iron men do not make good friends.

Pretending nothing is wrong does not make the valley go away. It simply results in procrastination—at best postponing the pain that eventually must be faced. Giants do not go away because we pretend they are not there, and delay typically only allows them to grow larger. Ironically, then, the macho approach can cause fear to grow. Fear keeps us from doing the things we know will help us. We know we should see a marriage counselor, but we try to tough it out until our marriage is almost gone.

Pain is like a warning light on a car dashboard. If the temperature light comes on, you know your car might be in danger of overheating. What do you do? Drive on, pretending there is no problem? Put a piece of masking tape over the light? No. You face the problem so it doesn't get worse.

Drugs, drinking and promiscuity are masking tape solutions—pain avoidance techniques. C. S. Lewis, the great British writer, said, "God whispers to us in our pleasures, speaks in our conscience, but shouts in our pain; it is His megaphone to rouse a deaf world."[1]

Trap #2—Try to escape.
Escaping is the Barney Fife approach. Why face a problem we can run away from? Perhaps if we get far enough away, we will never have to face it. Some people think changing jobs or moving to a new area will result in a fresh start without problems. Running from our problems, however, never helps. We hide out and run away, only to find later that the problem has not gone away.

David was tempted to try this approach when he was going through an especially scary time: "My heart is in anguish within me; the terrors of death assail me. Fear and trembling have beset me; horror has overwhelmed me" (Ps. 55:4–5). Did the great man of God simply rebuke the fear and take a stand for God? Well, yes, but not before fantasizing about escaping. "Oh, that I had the wings of a dove! I would fly away and be at rest—I would flee far away and stay in the desert; I would hurry to my place of shelter, far from the tempest and the storm" (vv. 6–8).

It is human nature to panic and run. We have all heard of the "fight or flight" instinct. When my congregation built our church building, we had to make sure all the chairs hooked together because if people panic, nobody wants chairs flying all over the place. Building and fire codes insist on such precautions. The gadgets that hook the chairs together are called "panic hardware."

People in panic can go to extremes to escape their situation. After many years of apparent stability, they may leave their families, their church or their country. Suicide is a radical attempt to escape, although it simply results in leaving our problems to others—often those we love the most and were hoping to help by our final action.

Television can be an escape. Movies, books, newspapers, certain friendships, the Internet, hobbies and theme parks—virtually anything can become an attempt to escape from the valley. But all such attempts to escape are doomed to fail, for you cannot run from yourself. At best, escape techniques offer temporary relief, a relief that quickly fades.

Trap #3—Be afraid.

Although David, like all of us, had an instinctive reaction of fear and a desire to escape from his troubles, he knew that was the wrong approach. An instinctive reaction of fear to a threatening situation does not disqualify us as people of faith—it simply means we are human. David overcame his fear and desire to flee, and instead he declared in faith, "But I call to God, and the LORD saves me.... Cast your cares on the LORD and he will sustain you; he will never let the righteous fall" (Ps. 55:16, 22).

Fear can stall our engines, freeze us in the headlights and even cause us to retreat. It is clearly one of the enemy's most successful and often used devices to stop us. But when we remember that God is with us, even in the valley, there is nothing in this life to be afraid of. Not death, not divorce, not business failure, not rebellious kids, not anything your imagination can conjure up.

Like David, Paul faced his share of life-threatening valleys.

> We do not want you to be uninformed, brothers, about the hardship we suffered in the province of Asia. We were under great pressure, far beyond our ability to endure, so that we despaired even of life. Indeed, in our hearts we felt the sentence of death. But this happened that we might not rely on ourselves but on God, who raises the dead. He has delivered us from such a deadly peril, and he will deliver us. On him we have set our hope that he will continue to deliver us.
> —2 CORINTHIANS 1:8–10

The apostle Paul, who found himself in a life-threatening situation, discovered that the saving power of God comes in three tenses—past, present and future. No matter when your hurt occurred, or will occur, God can still heal, save and deliver. Did you notice the three tenses in this passage? Paul says God *has* delivered us from such a deadly peril. He *is* delivering us. And on Him we have set our hope that He *shall yet* deliver us. Wherever we are in the valley—at the beginning, middle or end—there is no reason to fear. The same God who has saved us in the past is currently keeping us from falling. And there is no reason to fear the future, for with that track record we can know with certainty that He has not brought us this far to let us down now—or then.

Besides, what is the worst that can happen? Death? Even the threat of death did not bother Paul.

> For to me, to live is Christ and to die is gain. If I am to go on living in the body, this will mean fruitful labor for me. Yet what shall I choose? I do not know! I am torn between the two: I desire to depart and be with Christ, which is better by far; but it is more necessary for you that I remain in the body.
>
> —PHILIPPIANS 1:21–24

There is absolutely no way to defeat a guy who thinks like that—who knows the devil's trump card is not valid for the Christian. The believer is the only soldier in the world who dies and gets promoted!

STEPS TO TAKE

Step #1: Worry about nothing—pray about everything.

In light of such supreme confidence it is small wonder Paul goes on to note in Philippians 4:6–7, "Do not be anxious about anything, but in everything, by prayer and petition, with thanksgiving, present your requests to God. And the peace of God, which transcends all understanding, will guard your hearts and your minds in Christ Jesus."

Peter offers the same advice in 1 Peter 5:7: "Cast all your anxiety on him because he cares for you." Even when we are not in a valley and life is pretty good, we can find much to worry about. I consider myself a natural worrier. In fact, if there is nothing to worry about, I will find something. But one thing I have learned is that worry is a choice. The good news is that I have also learned I can choose not to worry—and instead choose to cast and throw all my worries on the Lord. And God does not play catch with my concerns. He never throws them back!

Fisherman are used to using lines and reels while casting for fish. God does not want us to use a reel with our worries. He tells us to cast our cares out and cut the line. Worry about nothing—pray about everything.

Worry is unreasonable. It causes us to see sandcastles as skyscrapers. It magnifies our troubles. Worst of all, it is a waste of time and energy. To worry about things we can do nothing about is a terrible waste of time. It accomplishes nothing. On the other hand, to worry about things we do have the power to change is wasted energy. Why not put that same effort into doing something to solve the problem? The bottom line is, we have choice. We can be worriers, wasting time and energy, or warriors, taking everything to the Lord in militant prayer.

Worry is unhealthy. It is a negative emotion that extracts a heavy toll on our bodies. Medical doctors will testify that many patients they see have ailments that originate in the mind, not the body. They can treat the symptoms all day long, but the root problem is mental, not physical, and must be treated as such. Our bodies were not made to worry. Anxiety costs too much.

Step #2: Remember that God is always there.

One of the scariest things about going through a valley is the nagging feeling that we are all alone. We feel naked, unprotected and vulnerable. But the fear is just that—only a feeling. The truth is that God has promised, "Never will I leave you; never will I forsake you" (Heb. 13:5). Jesus left us with the assurance, "And surely I am with you always, to the very end of the age" (Matt. 28:20).

David feared no evil while walking through the valley because he knew the Lord was with him no matter how he felt. He told the Lord, "Your rod and staff, they comfort me" (Ps. 23:4). David knew all about that. A shepherd's rod was a twenty-four-inch stick with a big knob at the end. In other words, it was a club, and in the hands of a skilled shepherd, it became a deadly weapon. No wolf or attacking animal was safe when the shepherd was wielding the club.

We receive that same kind of protection from the Lord. The rod represents His ability to safeguard us from attacks. With God we are never vulnerable.

The shepherd's staff was a long cane with a crook at the end. Shepherds used them to keep wandering sheep in line or to reach down and lift a fallen sheep out of a dangerous pit. Some of us are only alive and in church today because God used His staff to rescue us and to bring us back into the fold. God not only protects us from attack, but He also rescues us from our own mistakes.

God promises He will always do this, no matter how deep the valley or how dark the night. His staff is not short, His rod not weak, His love not diminished—He is well able to keep us through our darkest hour.

Step #3: Know you have not been rejected by God.

Rejection brings out the worst in us. It can cause us to feel unloved, unwanted and unworthy. Here are some typical symptoms:

- You have low self-esteem.
- You have a habit of comparing yourself to others.
- You frequently put yourself down.
- You expect people not to like you.
- You have a fear of not doing things right.

GOD NEVER WASTES A HURT

- You place undue emphasis on the way you look.
- You are motivated by what other people think about you.
- You have an eating disorder.
- You are hurt and depressed.
- You are a bottomless pit of emotional need.

God is not the author of rejection. God never rejects a sincere heart. Scripture says, "Him that cometh to me I will in no wise cast out" (John 6:37, KJV). Oftentimes we create God in our image. We project onto Him our insecurities as well as the negative perceptions of others. "No one thinks I'm any good, including me—I just know God feels the same way." Thus, it is easy for us to think God rejects us. "Why not? Everybody else does."

Such thinking is simply another misconception that keeps us needlessly wandering in a valley. It prolongs the misery and deepens the agony—and all because, like Adam and Eve, we believe a lie. It is a lie that any of us are rejected by God, and if that thought is bothering you, make a point of memorizing parts of the Bible that remind you of the many promises you have through Christ. He is yours, and you are His, and nothing can separate you from His love and acceptance. Nothing.

Step # 4: Let setbacks become comebacks.

There is a story about a mule that fell into a deep, dry well. His owner, believing that the mule was fatally injured and that there was no hope of getting it out anyway, decided that the humane thing was to bury it. So he brought a truckload of dirt and began dumping it into the well. However, the mule had indeed survived the fall, and as the wheelbarrows full of dirt came down, the old mule would simply shake the dust off his head, and with a "heehaw," stomp the dirt under his feet. With each stomp he was raised a few inches. This continued

104

all day long, until eventually, with one last shake of his head, one last "heehaw" and one last stomp, he casually stepped out of the well.

What might have killed him proved to be the means for his deliverance. God specializes in turning the very thing that hurts into the means of our rescue. When you have a setback, don't take a step back; get ready for your comeback.

Step #5: Live one day at a time.

When you are in the middle of a valley, already feeling tired and completely worn out, the thought of making it to the end seems overwhelming. Assessing the situation, it becomes obvious that victory, while certain, will not come easily or quickly. "How can I go on? I don't think I have the energy or strength to make it to the end." Today has as many challenges as we can handle. To even think about tomorrow would crush our spirits.

When a task seems overwhelming, it is best to take things one step at a time. The old adage is true—how do you eat an elephant? One bite at a time. The key to making it over the long haul is to stay focused on the task at hand. Jesus said it like this:

> Therefore, do not worry about tomorrow, for tomorrow will worry about itself. Each day has enough trouble of its own.
>
> —MATTHEW 6:34

Anyone who has been in a recovery program like Alcoholics Anonymous knows the importance of taking life day by day, even minute by minute. The thought of never again taking a drink, having a smoke or living life without a "rush" seems overwhelming. It is too much to ask for. But staying sober for the next sixty seconds is doable. Stay focused, then, on the next minute, then the next…then the next. Before you know it, an hour has passed, then a day, then a week and so on.

Quick fixes are rare. In the newspaper I saw a sampling of seminars that are being held around Los Angeles. They included:

- "How to write a movie in twenty-one days"
- "How to write a novel in three weeks or less"
- "Begin speaking a new language confidently in three hours"
- "Success and happiness and prosperity in five minutes a day"

Such promises!

I heard a joke about a hillbilly family who took a trip to the city. They had never seen modern civilization before, so everything was new to them. When they pulled up to the hotel, Dad parked the car. "You wait here," Dad told Mom. "Junior and I will check things out."

They walked inside and were dazzled by the sights. Lights, music and bellhops rushing here and there—it was more than they could take in all at once.

Then they noticed the elevators, but they had no idea what they were. All they could see were doors sliding open, people entering and then the same doors sliding shut. A wrinkled old woman walked up slowly, pushed a button and walked in, doors closing behind her. A few minutes later, the doors opened again, and out walked a beautiful and shapely young woman. After a moment, Dad turned to his son and said, "Hey, Junior, go git Mama."

If only change were so easy!

By taking life one day at a time, you allow God to change you on His schedule. Do not try to set the pace because you will only frustrate yourself. Do not think about tomorrow's troubles, and do not take out your umbrella before it starts raining. You have to decide to make it one more day. You have to decide to take one more step. Pretty soon you find yourself walking through the valley of the shadow of death and fearing no evil. You decide not to worry, and now you are making it one step at a time. The end is finally in sight.

Everyone goes through valleys. We go through them for any number of reasons. But God never asks us to camp out there forever. Though at times it seems as if they will never end, they are a temporary part of God's total purpose for our lives. Weeping may endure for a night, but joy comes in the morning. Even the hurtful, painful stuff we go through can become the threads He uses to weave a gorgeous fabric. The end result works for our benefit—and the benefit of others. Will you let Him?

In the next section we will look at what to do as we prepare to leave the valley behind.

❧

Section II
Leaving the Valley Behind

Chapter 6

If You Stay Here, You Will Die

R od was flying home when the small plane he had hired
malfunctioned, causing the engine to stall. Trees brushed
the belly of the plane, and the ground moved very quickly
beneath them. Several buzzers went off, and Rod knew they
were going to crash.

He was sitting next to the plane's only door, and when the
plane slammed into the ground, the door flew off and Rod
was thrown from the plane. He felt himself hit the ground,
getting a mouthful of dirt, and then everything turned black
as he lost consciousness.

As he lay there in what felt like a deep sleep, he heard a
voice speaking to him. It said, "If you stay here, you will
die."

Rod answered the voice in his mind, "I can't die. I have all
these things to do. I am still young. I've got my family."

The voice repeated, "If you stay here, you will die."

Immediately, Rod's senses began to return. He heard the
fire crackling around him, smelled the stench of the weeds
and the brush burning and then felt flames licking his own

flesh. He finally saw that flames were everywhere. He knew that, to survive, he needed to move quickly. He breathed a prayer, "Lord, give me the strength to get out of here, and give me direction to know where to go." Somehow, some way, he garnered the strength to move away from the deadly flames.

The plane crash was discovered, and Rod was airlifted to a hospital with burns covering one-fourth of his body. Only he survived the crash.

Rod recovered rapidly, and he was soon back at work and in church. He bears a few visible scars from the harrowing experience, but he believes God spared his life. The scars serve as a reminder of the miracle.

The most remarkable thing about that story to me is how Rod heard that voice telling him to leave the place of danger. I believe it was the voice of God speaking to him, saying, "If you stay here, you will die."

Although not many of us, thankfully, have been through a situation as traumatic as a plane crash, many of us have been through a few crash-and-burn situations in life. The abuse, misuse and hurts of our past can be just as real and at times even as deadly as a plane crash. The scar and wounds we carry, though not visible, are just as real. Like Rod, we need to get up and move on with our lives. From the flames of the past God is trying to get our attention, saying, "If you stay here, you will die."

Ezekiel 37 talks about a valley full of bones. It is a place where life had once flourished, but now only decaying remnants remain. It is a valley of broken dreams, missed opportunities and shattered goals. While valleys certainly can teach great lessons and offer wonderful fruit, they are never meant to be permanent. Tents may be pitched, but houses should not be built. We have been talking about the valleys

God takes us through, those we put ourselves through and those others put us through. Regardless of why we are in the valley, God expects us to *grow* through them, not just go through them. Jesus Himself was led into the wilderness by the Spirit to be tempted by the devil—a perfect portrait of a valley experience.

But there comes a time to leave the valley behind. Lessons have been learned and the supernatural provision of God has been real, but it is now time to move on. What if Jesus had stayed in the desert instead of starting His ministry? Not only would He have missed the plan of God for His own life, but He would have also thwarted God's strategy to save humanity. What if you stay in the valley when God wants you to move? You will die, and perhaps God's plan to use you to touch others will die with you.

In the famous passage in Ezekiel 37 about the valley of dry bones, God gives Ezekiel a prophecy about the restoration of the nation of Israel. Many Bible scholars see Israel's birth as a nation in 1948 as fulfilling that prophecy. But there is also an application of that verse for the subject that we are dealing with.

Ezekiel 37:1 says:

> The hand of the LORD was upon me, and he brought me out by the Spirit of the LORD and set me in the middle of the valley; it was full of bones. He led me back and forth among them, and I saw a great many bones on the floor of the valley, bones that were very dry.

The symbol here is of complete, abject death. This is beyond rotting corpses and the stench of decay. No flesh, no maggots and no creepy, crawling things that would make us scream if this were some horror movie. Death and decomposition have reigned for so long that even the remaining bones are dry and brittle. The scorching sun of this valley has bleached them, and by all appearances there is no chance of life.

DID YOUR DREAMS DIE IN THE VALLEY?

When I read this passage, I get a picture of someone who has been through a devastating valley—so devastating that no sign of life appears, only the hapless remains of what would have been, could have been and should have been. Upon reaching the end of the valley, he begins to assess what has happened. I see a person making his way through piles of bones, picking them up, trying to remember what their function used to be. I see the tears form and the regret well up inside his chest. I see him counting what was lost:

- Relationships
- Family
- Finances
- Honor
- Self-respect

Some of you are walking out of a valley and thinking, "I don't see any fruit from what I've gone through. I see lifeless bones."

Did your dream die in the valley? Did you lose it all? Some of you are wondering whether there is hope for your marriage, business or physical body. The worst has passed, but you have been left with nothing. Why go on when everything you were counting on lies dead on the valley floor?

Everything may seem to be gone, but one thing remains—our ability and freedom to respond. We have options when we begin to leave the valley God has taken us through.

"Forget it!"

Some people hang up the cleats and walk off the field: "Enough living for God! I get hurt every time I try to do something good for Him."

There are plenty of people who take that option, but it never leads anywhere. In the end, the pain will be worse without God than with Him, no matter how much we endure in following Him. Remember, failure is never final, and it is always too soon to quit.

"After what I've been through, I'm not worthy to help others."

Some people stay in the family of God, but they disqualify themselves from service. They have not exactly quit, but they consider themselves useless. As we will see, this is exactly the opposite of what God has in mind.

"Someone will pay for what I've been through."

Some people become consumed by their pain, often after the pain itself is long gone. Scars are meant to be trophies, but that is different than flaunting our hurts and inflicting long stories of injustice on those around us. When people talk too much about their hurts, it sometimes means they have not yet found resolution for them and are still being weighed down by resentment.

"Don't touch me there, God."

Some people sincerely want to continue loving God, but they won't allow Him to address their area of hurt. They refuse to talk about it to others, and they would rather pretend nothing ever happened. In a way, they are denying that their dream died. Instead of walking out of the valley and seeing God resurrect their dream on the other side, they stay where they are, silently weeping over its grave.

"Trying hard to serve God just doesn't pay."

Those who have been hurt in a ministry setting know this response well. They feel burned by Christians and sapped of their enthusiasm for the work of the Lord. They know in their hearts that God's way is the only way, but they convince themselves that the ministry is too corrupted by bad politics or dishonest people. Having given up on ministry, they hang around as do-nothing Christians, well versed in biblical matters, but unwilling to get involved.

MISCONCEPTIONS ABOUT GOD

Valleys can warp our perception of God, even when we are sincerely following Christ. Subtly, wrong notions or observations that we may mistake for wisdom can influence our view.

We may see God as a cosmic kill-joy, a dream-destroyer whose favorite word is "no." We may think:

- God puts too many unattainable demands on our life.
- He wants us to be bored, because fun is sinful.
- He wants strict obedience because of a divine desire to control.

We may also come to believe that God does not care for us in a personal way. We may feel disconnected, distant and cold toward the things of God, and we may interpret this as God separating from us. If He is there at all, He must be too busy to really know us personally.

We may see Him as a God who lets us down, who is inconsistent and who does not live up to His Word.

We may see Him as a God who is never happy with us—a God whose expectations are so high that He is, in the end, unpleasable. If so, why even try?

When we are feeling and doing good, such misconceptions are rare. But when we are in a dry valley, crazy thoughts can mislead us like a mirage. Our only line of defense is the clear declaration of Scripture. A multitude of verses refute these foolish ideas. Psalm 34:10 says that those who seek the Lord lack no good thing.

Psalm 84:11 says, "No good thing does he withhold from those whose walk is blameless."

First Timothy 6:17 says that God "richly provides us with everything for our enjoyment."

First Peter 5:7 says, "Cast all your anxiety on him because he cares for you."

Psalm 34:18 says, "The LORD is close to the broken-hearted and saves those who are crushed in spirit."

Especially when we hurt, or when our dreams have been dashed, we need to remember that God is still there and that He still cares. He has neither forgotten us nor abandoned us. When all hope seems to have vanished a long time ago, as in the valley of dry bones, we must remember that we serve a God who can bring good out of bad, order out of chaos, light out of darkness and life out of death. Our deepest hurts and pains can become the very material for better dreams, better hopes and a better life.

USES FOR PAIN

Who likes pain? Nobody. But pain has a use. If Rod had not felt the fire burning his skin, he probably would have stayed where he was and died. God used the pain to get him to move.

The absence of pain is actually a sign of death, not life. I remember as a youth hearing a song about a guy who had been hurt so often in life and love that he was throwing in the towel. He was never going to risk loving or really living again; he was going to live his life as an island—never experiencing hurt or pain again. But in so doing, he would also never experience the joy and happiness that life and love can offer.

Pharmaceutical companies spend countless millions testing and marketing pain-relievers. Nevertheless, try as we might to avoid it, pain is a companion to every human at one time or another. But what is pain good for?

Pain gets our attention.

Some of us will only go to the dentist when the pain in our mouths overcomes our fear of the dentist's drill. We may know we need the work done, but that knowledge alone does not get us to act. Pain is a cattle prod and a teacher's rod. In general, people do not change when they see the light, but when they feel the heat.

It was the pain of hunger that caused the prodigal son to come home. Only after the pain had gained his attention did he realize his lifestyle was not only decadent, but it was fruitless. Pain preceded a change of direction, and it led him to repentance.

Pain trains.

Pain instills wisdom. It teaches us where not to go and what not to do. The nerve endings God placed on the tips of our fingers teach us that fire is hot and can burn. Pain is part of the curriculum of school we all attend—the University of Hard Knocks.

Like any good parent, God would prefer we listen to His instructions and so avoid a lot of hurt, but He has no problem allowing us to learn for ourselves if we are insistent. The psalmist, perhaps reluctantly, had to confess in Psalm 119:71, "It was good for me to be afflicted so that I might learn your decrees."

Pain tests character.

Some of us do not know what we are made of until it is

revealed in a painful situation. We may think we have overcome our tendency to have a foul mouth until we hit our finger with the hammer. I have heard it said people are like toothpaste; we never know what is really inside until squeezed. We are like tea bags. We do not know what is inside us until we are in hot water.

Isaiah 48:10 says, "See, I have refined you, though not as silver; I have tested you in the furnace of affliction."

Pain protects.

Pain can protect us from further or even more severe pain. Sometimes pain reveals something worse than pain: fever, illness, injury or infection. If we respond to the pain, we avoid worse consequences.

The pain of depression, for example, can lead us to get the help we need, thereby avoiding further pain and possibly the tragedy of suicide. Pain is typically the result of a symptom shouting to us that something somewhere is wrong. Hopefully, that can lead to the treatment and cure of the root problem.

In the Middle East, shepherds would occasionally break the leg of a rebellious sheep and carry it on their shoulders. During the healing process, the sheep would learn the shepherd's voice and not to wander off. The pain of a broken leg was better than the pain of falling victim to a wolf or dying of exposure all alone in the wilderness.

Pain produces growth.

Bodybuilders used to wear shirts that proclaimed, "No Pain, No Gain." Trainers will tell you that it is the last few bench presses—the ones that are extremely difficult and seem to burn—that really allow muscle development to take place. Every child has experienced some form of "growing pains."

The same is true in our spiritual growth. The apostle James noted in James 1:3 that, like resistance training, trials produce strength and perseverance. Hebrews 12:11 states, "No discipline seems pleasant at the time, but painful. Later on, however, it produces a harvest of righteousness and peace for those who have been trained by it." Handled properly, pain can eventually lead to great maturity. The truth is that some of us will never learn that God is all we need until God is all we have.

THEM BONES SHALL RISE AGAIN

God posed this question to Ezekiel. "Son of man, can these bones live?" (Ezek. 37:3).

Is God asking you the same question today? In the midst of a marriage that is dead, is God asking, "Can this marriage live again?" While Chapter 11 is being filed, is God asking, "Can this business be restored?" Can our dead dreams or our long-forgotten hopes yet live? Can they possibly be reborn? Do we believe He can restore life, or do we choose another option?

Ezekiel responded, "O Sovereign LORD, you alone know" (v. 3). That is the same response we would probably give. "God, why are You asking me? Only You know whether or not the bones of my marriage or the remains of my business can live again."

God then gave Ezekiel an answer that we need to grab hold of. He said, "Prophesy to these bones" (v. 4). To prophesy means to speak forth the Word of God in a given situation. Instead of talking about your troubles or complaining about your burdens, why not allow the life-giving power of God's Word to come out of your mouth? Choose the option that can bring life. You do not have to be a prophet, pastor or trained theologian to get a word from the Lord.

I want to challenge you to prophesy to your valleys. Speak the Word of the Lord into the canyons and crevices through which you have been wandering. Maybe you have been waiting for God to act, and God has been waiting for you to speak. When you sense the deliverance of the Lord at hand, turn around and shout to your valley, "Your time is up! What the devil meant for harm, God will arrange for my good, and I will not stay here one day beyond God's appointed time."

Ezekiel obeyed and declared the words that the Spirit of the Lord had given him:

> Then he said to me, "Prophesy to these bones and say to them, 'Dry bones, hear the word of the LORD! This is what the Sovereign LORD says to these bones: I will make breath enter you, and you will come to life. I will attach tendons to you and make flesh come upon you and cover you with skin; I will put breath in you, and you will come to life. Then you will know that I am the LORD.'" So I prophesied as I was commanded.
>
> —EZEKIEL 37:4–7

I will say it again—stop complaining about your valley and start prophesying to it. If you do not know where to start, simply look in the mirror and prophesy to yourself. How? By speaking and reminding yourself of the promises of God.

- "I can do all things through Christ who strengthens me."
- "Greater is He that is in me than He that is in the world."
- "I am more than a conqueror in Christ Jesus."
- "I do unto others as I would have them do unto me."
- "I forgive so that my Father in heaven can forgive me."
- "I seek the Lord, and He answers me and delivers me from all my fears."
- "I am a child of God. I am more than a conqueror. I am a chosen person. I am a holy race. I am the head and not the tail."

Prophesy to your children, "You are an overcoming child of God. I am so proud of you."

There comes a time to get out of the valley—for if you stay there, you will die. There comes a time when speaking the promises of the Word is not faith babble; it is the creative power of God working miraculously through you. With faith, courage and the timing of God, the same thing that happened with Ezekiel will happen with you:

> And as I was prophesying, there was a noise, a rattling sound, and the bones came together, bone to bone. I looked, and tendons and flesh appeared on them and skin covered them, but there was no breath in them.
> —EZEKIEL 37:7–8

Notice that good things are happening, but the transformation is not yet complete. A life, a marriage or a business does not fall apart overnight, nor does a healing miracle take place without tenacity. Praying once or speaking once is not always enough. The structure of a good marriage may have returned—you are finally living in the same house and attending church together again. But until the spark of love is restored, the process is not finished. Until it is, everything is still on shaky ground. You need to develop a lifestyle of prophesying to your valleys and low places. Keep pressing on until the breath of life returns.

> Then he said to me, "Prophesy to the breath; prophesy, son of man, and say to it, 'This is what the Sovereign LORD says: Come from the four winds, O breath, and breathe into these slain, that they may live.'" So I prophesied as he commanded me, and breath entered them; they came to life and stood up on their feet—a vast army.
> —EZEKIEL 37:9–10

Your dreams can live again, even if they seem dead. God specializes in raising armies out of dry bones.

If You Stay Here, You Will Die

JOSEPH

We have talked about how unfairly Joseph was treated by his family in a previous chapter. Still, Joseph kept his dream alive against all odds.

By way of a reminder, Joseph was from a very dysfunctional family—four mothers, one father and a pack of brothers who seemed to know no bounds in their sin. Things did not get any easier for him once he left (or better yet, was forced from) his home. Along the way to his becoming Egypt's *de facto* leader was every Hollywood plot device ever invented: intrigue, sex, incest, murder plots, sexual harassment, false charges and finally redemption.

Joseph's story removes any excuse we could have for not dreaming, even under the most devastating of circumstances. Like Joseph, each of us is a potential overcomer, world-shaker and history-maker, no matter what our background is like.

When Joseph was born, his father favored him, probably because he came by Rachel, the woman he had worked fourteen years for and loved. Maybe Joseph looked like Rachel. Rachel died giving birth to her next son, Benjamin. So it might be that not only was Joseph the son of Jacob's old age, as the Bible says, but that when Jacob looked at Joseph he saw the woman he had loved.

Though Jacob is one of the patriarchs of the faith, if you turned on any daytime talk show, you could not find a worse situation than the one that existed in his family. At one point, Reuben, the oldest, slept with one of his dad's wives, not just for lustful reasons, but because he was the oldest son and was declaring that he wanted the family fortune early. He was trying to step into a prominence and authority in the family that was not yet his to claim.

Then there was Judah, the father of the tribe by the same name. Jesus is from this tribe—He is "the Lion of the tribe of

Judah." The word *Jew* comes from Judah's name. You would think that the father of such a prodigious genealogical line would be a saint, but Joseph's brother Judah had his share of scandals. Genesis 38 records an escapade he had with a prostitute that reads like the most titillating, if disgusting, kind of soap opera.

Joseph had clear dreams about his future, but he did not foresee the major series of challenges he would have to face before his dreams came true. Between every promise and provision are problems. Joseph was like many of the young people I see to whom God has given a great vision or dream. God seldom allows them to see the cost that will go along with it. Perhaps He doesn't want to discourage them before they ever get started!

Joseph's first dream was of him and his brothers in a field harvesting grain, and his brothers' sheaves bowed down to Joseph's sheaf. His second dream depicted the sun, moon and eleven stars, representing his mother, father and brothers, bowing down to him.

His brothers hated him because of his dreams and because of his father's preferential treatment of him. As we saw in the first section, they cruelly planned to kill him, but then sold him into slavery.

Can you imagine keeping your dream alive in the bottom of a dry cistern?

How about riding through the desert with a caravan of traders with no scruples?

Let me tell you, Joseph could have kept a cistern mentality after he was let out. He could have cried all the way to Egypt and a long time after that. He could have pulled people aside: "Hi, I'm Joseph, and I've really had it bad. Let me tell you what my brothers did to me."

But Joseph knew that if he stayed there in his mind, he

would die. He may have been in one valley after another, but he did not linger there when God called him on.

Some people want a testimony without the test, a message without the mess and the provision without the problem. But others end up wanting the test without the testimony, the mess without the message and the problem without the provision. They become attached to their hurts with the sticky glue of bitterness.

They trade their dreams for seeds of resentment.

How High Can You Bounce?

At what point do you give up your dreams? How quickly do you snap under pressure?

I love golf, and having played with people young and old, I have learned that it does not take much strength to send the ball a good distance. Why? Because a golf ball is made to be resilient. Inside is string wound tight so that the ball flies off the head of your club.

If you put a golf ball in the freezer long enough, it will lose all of its bounce. In fact, if you freeze a golf ball cold enough, it will shatter when it is hit. A simple environmental change causes the ball to act entirely different than it was made to act.

That is a picture of some people. Life has turned their hearts cold. The valley of the shadow of death has stolen their warmth. Dry and brittle bones do not bounce—they break! And now they no longer bounce back either. Maybe they hit the ground with a thud; maybe they even shatter.

How high can you bounce? Have you lost your resilience? Have you quit hitting back when life hits you with stuff?

Have you given up the dream God gave you?

The good news is that a frozen golf ball can be thawed out, and once defrosted it will bounce as high as ever. You can bounce back, too! No matter how hard and brittle you may have become, the Holy Spirit specializes in warming your heart until once again you have a glide in your stride and a skip in your step. The Bible says God can give you a new heart, and you will bounce back stronger than ever.

If your hurts are still so tender that the last thing you want to do is bounce, God has a very gentle way of bringing restoration and renewal. In speaking of the coming Messiah, Isaiah predicted:

> A bruised reed he will not break, and a smoldering wick
> he will not snuff out.
>
> —ISAIAH 42:3

The image is of a bent piece of straw and of a candle that is almost out—just a little glow. Both are delicate. Have you ever tried to straighten a bent piece of straw? No matter how careful you are, you will likely end up breaking it. Or how about a candle that is virtually out with only a slight glow remaining? If you do not give it enough breath, it will go out completely. If you blow too hard to bring the flame back to life, you may snuff it out.

Sometimes that is how we are, especially coming out of a long and difficult valley. The best efforts of others are either too strong or not strong enough. We are fragile, sensitive and almost dead. It was said of Humpty Dumpty, "All the king's horses and all the king's men could not put Humpty Dumpty back together again." But what the best efforts of doctors, therapists and even pastors cannot do, Jesus the Messiah can do. He has just the right touch. He can breathe on the smoldering wick and straighten the bent reed.

He will not kill your dreams. In fact, many times He is the only One who can keep them alive.

Paul talked about how his dreams were almost lost. He says in 2 Corinthians 4:8–9:

If You Stay Here, You Will Die

We are hard pressed on every side, but not crushed...

Have you ever felt like that? Everywhere you turn there is bad news. Things are bad at home. Things are bad at work. To make matters worse, even your golf game is at an all-time low. But it is not funny. You are surrounded by pressure. It feels as if the walls are closing in on you. Still, as Paul notes, by the grace of God you are not yet crushed.

Perplexed, but not in despair...

Even the great apostle was at times confused: *Why did this happen to me? I don't understand this.* As Christians we do not always have all the answers. But we do not have to despair, because we at least know the Answer.

Persecuted, but not abandoned . . .

Persecution is almost always unfair. Harassment, discrimination and prejudice remain facts of life. Like Joseph before him, Paul knew that if everyone forsook him, God would never leave him alone.

Struck down, but not destroyed.

The first *Rocky* movie was, in my opinion, the best one. Some of you might think that strange, since it was the only one where Rocky lost. Well, he may have lost the fight, but as they say, he won the war. In this first film Rocky is selected as a patsy for Apollo Creed, a Muhammad Ali-type character. The fight is supposed to be more of a spectacle than a real fight, with Rocky, the Italian Stallion, being the Great White Hope.

To the surprise of all involved, the patsy ends up giving Apollo Creed the fight of his life. Creed eventually wins the fight, but not before Rocky takes him the full length. Battered and beaten, Rocky keeps getting up off the mat and is actually getting in quite a few good licks himself when the final bell sounds.

One scene I will never forget is when Rocky is on the mat being counted out by the referee. His opponent is prancing triumphantly around the ring, when all of a sudden he turns around to see Rocky yet again getting up. Creed gives him this look that says, "I can't believe it! What am I going to have to do to knock this guy down and keep him down?"

That is how the devil ought to start looking at us. Rocky would not give up his dream, even when he felt hard pressed, perplexed, persecuted and struck down. We too ought to bounce back every time the devil knocks us down. We may occasionally be knocked down, but we are never knocked out. Paul had his share of "light and momentary struggles," most of which would make us shudder. But no matter what hit him, he bobbed to the surface. He stood up one more time. He refused to be defeated. He held to the dream God had given him.

What dream do you have? Do you remember when you were a kid, thinking of what you could accomplish when you got older? God has a dream for you just as He had a dream for Joseph, but what does it take to knock you out? The difference between those who make it and those who don't is that those who make it refuse to dwell in the valley or go down for the count.

Chapter 7

Your Problem Is Not Your Problem

W hat should we do?" yelled Helene. "I don't know," I screamed. The kitchen ceiling looked as if it would soon catch on fire. Our good friend Helene was trying to teach my wife, Marguerite, and me how to cook Brazilian doughnuts when the oil became too hot and caught on fire.

In the panic of the moment, we looked more like the Three Stooges than three adults. Marguerite grabbed the handle of the pan and yelled for me to open the sliding glass door that led to our backyard. It was just a few steps away from the kitchen. That was a BIG mistake. We forgot one important thing. Because we live on a hill, there is usually a slight breeze blowing against our house.

The moment Marguerite took a step outside, the wind blew the hot flames onto her hand. She instantly dropped the pan, spilling cooking oil and flames everywhere. Fortunately nothing caught on fire, and the flames quickly died down.

Her right hand, though, was horribly burnt. It looked melted, like a wax figure from one of those horror movies.

Marguerite was also seven months pregnant with our first child. When I saw my wife's hand, I did what most young husbands do—completely panic!

While Marguerite calmly used her left hand to put ice into a bowl and plunged her melting hand into it, I was trying to call emergency (this was in the days before 911). I kept getting the wrong number—I distinctly remember at one point making contact with Toys 'R Us, although this was no time for shopping for our new child. I was so useless that Marguerite eventually had to grab the phone with her remaining good hand and call the hospital herself.

Though we laugh now, it was not so funny at the time. Marguerite was referred to one of the top burn specialists in the world. Fortunately, skin grafting wasn't necessary as was initially diagnosed—God did a miracle—and she was able to regain full use of her right hand. But scars remained, and the most noticeable ones were not on her hand.

For years even a romantic fireplace could trigger painful memories and present fears. The invisible wounds were just as real as the physical ones. How could a silly cooking accident leave such a lasting imprint?

Valleys we go through commonly leave lingering hurts and bruises. Even the church is full of emotionally wounded people, and every wound is different. Some have been cleaned, bandaged and healed. You would never know a hurt ever existed. Others are infected and still painful to the touch. Some wounds have actually become a source of encouragement and healing for others, while some wounds yield only bitterness.

Some people let go; others hang on. A few hold on to so much trash from the past that they should be driving garbage trucks, not BMWs.

Some wounds leave scars. I have a scar on my forehead

from a skin cancer I had, before lasers could do a neater job of removing it. What does that scar remind me of? The cancer? The possibility that my life might have been in jeopardy? No. It reminds me of the grace of God. He spared me, and I am thankful.

What do you think of when you see your scars? Do you relive the pain? Do you feel the hurt as if it happened yesterday? Do you turn away from God?

WHY SCARS?

An immensely popular television show of late is *Survivor*. Though I missed every episode, I am told that over twenty million people a week tuned in to see who would win a million dollars for being the last one standing, so to speak. Scars are evidence that we are survivors in real life, and the rewards can be far greater than a bundle of cash.

A famous survivor in the Old Testament was a man named Jacob. From his birth, the odds were stacked against him, but he always found a way to come out on top. His name means "supplanter," or "he who strives with man." His twin brother, Esau, came out of the womb first, but Jacob was grabbing at his heel, as if to foreshadow their later struggles for the birthright.

Jacob did indeed wrestle the birthright from his brother, Esau. It was not done by brute physical strength, for Esau was the strong, outdoors kind of guy. Jacob was more of a thinker, a scheming sort of man who probably thought he could get along fine without the help of others. He would out-think his opponent and scheme his way around obstacles.

God, however, had plans to teach Jacob a lesson. One night He appeared to him as the angel of the Lord, which most Bible scholars believe is the preincarnate Christ, and wrestled with him all night. Jacob was no longer striving with man—he was striving with God. Though the struggle lasted all night, Jacob was tenacious and would not let go. Like a toddler wrestling with his dad, Jacob had no chance of winning. Every clever move only brought frustration, and every scheme ended up a dead-end street. He was learning that he could not get everything in life through his own smarts. He was learning what it is like to wrestle with God.

At least Jacob didn't quit, and the experience radically changed him. God even gave him a new name—Israel—"he who strives and prevails with God." Before Jacob had been like a hard-nosed businessman. He was able to swim with the sharks and survive. Now he discovered his power came from utter dependence upon the Lord. As a symbol of this, the Bible says God touched him in the bone of his hip, giving him a limp—a lifelong, visible reminder that it is not by might, nor by human power or ingenuity, but by God's Spirit that the will of God is accomplished. (See Genesis 25:21–32:32.)

PROBLEM—OR OPPORTUNITY?

Jacob's macho strut had been literally replaced with a humble limp. No longer could he glide through life looking the picture of self-confidence. I am sure his limp bothered him now and then; it perhaps even caused him to modify some of his activities. I doubt it bothered him too much, however, for it was a living memorial to a new and better way of living. Jacob was a changed man. Maybe he limped with men, but he now walked with God.

Troubles and problems are often God's appointed agents for our success. The wounds and scars we carry out of these experiences can be viewed as either scarlet letters of shame or honorable marks of distinction. The choice we make is crucial, for it not only affects how we view our past, but how we will live in the future.

Your Problem Is Not Your Problem

Let me share a secret with you: Your problem is not your problem; the way you see your problem is your problem. Is it a scar or a star? An unlucky break or an opportunity for something fresh and new? A burden or a blessing?

My wife is one of those incredible people who instinctively see problems as opportunities to grow. Unfortunately, I have to work hard at this. I am much more prone to expect things to go wrong, so when they do, it simply confirms what I suspected.

For example, I remember one Saturday night when we were reviewing a videotaped testimony we were planning to use in the next morning's service. Sure enough, the video player didn't work. Not exactly an earth-shattering problem, right? Nevertheless I instantly went into my typical rant: "See, I knew this would happen. Something always goes wrong (remember Murphy's law?), even with all the planning we do. If only we had state-of-the-art equipment."

Talk about a golf ball with no resilience! A bad situation hits—a small one at that—and I thud to the ground. No bounce whatsoever.

Marguerite, on the other hand, looked at things from a different perspective, "Well, thank God we found out tonight. Let's see if someone knows how to fix it." As usual, she was right, and things went smoothly the following day. Not only that, but during the entire process of getting help she was calm, cool and collected. I was tense, hot and falling apart—all over a silly video player.

The video player that wouldn't work was not my problem. How I viewed the situation was my problem. I wish I were more like Marguerite, naturally bent to look for the lessons learned and the options available. But I am not. I have to make a conscious decision every day to bounce and not break. I am not yet as good as Marguerite, and maybe I never will be, but I am better than I used to be. The old nature is strong and wants to see problems as problems, not as opportunities.

Paul was a master at seeing opportunities in the most challenging of circumstances. He was thrown in jail more times than I can count, but instead of moping around in chains, he introduced the jailers to Christ. We know this because when he wrote the epistle to the Philippians, he made a casual closing comment that is actually very poignant: "All the saints send you greetings, especially those who belong to Caesar's household" (Phil. 4:22). History confirms that Nero had one of his wives executed because she was a Christian. Though physically in chains, Paul's ministry reached into the backyard of the most powerful man on the planet at that time.

Paul bounced back. He saw opportunities even through the bars of a Roman prison. Paul must have led a guard to Christ, who led a friend to Christ, who led another friend to Christ...until it reached Caesar's own house. This reminds of an old television commercial where a lady said, "I told two people, and they told two people...and so on, and so on, and so on," and the screen divided and multiplied into a hundred squares.

That is what happens when we see problems as opportunities. The gospel gets plenty of room to multiply.

CORRECT GUIDANCE COMES FROM GOD

You haven't forgotten about the saga of Joseph yet, have you? Having been sold into slavery in Egypt, Joseph was faithfully serving his master Potiphar. Potiphar's wife, a wealthy Egyptian socialite, could not help but notice the attractive young servant, and she tried her best to seduce him. Joseph was thrown into prison when the wife, angry that he had rebuffed all her advances, lied and said he had forced himself on her. This was yet another of those occasions where Joseph did the right thing—and received a criminal's punishment. And yet he did not see the problem as the sum of his situation. How do we know this? Because the Bible says he gained favor with the jailers and was put in charge of the goings-on in prison. You know the old saying— you can't keep a good man down.

You do not gain favor by having a pity party. You do it by continuing on with your dream—no matter how bleak things appear.

It was in prison that Joseph met two men who had displeased Pharaoh.

> Each of the two men—the cupbearer and the baker of the king of Egypt, who were being held in prison—had a dream the same night, and each dream had a meaning of its own.
>
> —GENESIS 40:5

In the ancient world, particularly in Egypt and Babylon, people believed that dreams (and constellations and other things) were tools of the gods to speak to humans. In this case, that was true.

The cupbearer dreamed that a vine grew three branches, which budded and blossomed. A cluster of grapes appeared, and he grabbed the grapes, squeezed them in a cup and gave the wine to Pharaoh.

The cupbearer did not know what his dream meant, and apparently this wasn't just a passing fancy because it disturbed him. He sensed there was some meaning in the dream, but he did not know how to interpret it.

The baker too had a dream. He had three baskets on his head, and in the top basket was a bunch of bread, and the birds came down and pecked it all up. He too was puzzled by his dream.

Joseph noticed that the men were bothered by their dreams, and he said to them, "Do not interpretations belong to God?" (Gen. 40:8).

This is an important question for you and me. Why do some people see only problems while others see opportunities? Why do some bounce while others break? The key may be found in whom we allow to interpret the events of our lives.

Who filters our thoughts and opinions?

Whom do we allow to influence our perspective on life?

Friends?

Relatives?

Television preachers?

Prophets?

Psychics?

More than a few professing Christians mess around with the astrology section of the newspaper, and even though they claim it is all in good fun, they really do take it seriously at some level. And some people who have named Christ as their Lord do call psychic hotlines. Sad as it seems, it is a fact.

I read a few years back that the largest psychic hotline went bankrupt. The newspaper report quoted them as saying something like, "We did not foresee certain conditions."

I read that and thought, *You are going to take people's money when they call, and you can't even foresee certain conditions that are going to take your whole business down?*

As Joseph would say, "Do not correct interpretations belong to God?"

If you are tempted to involve yourself in things like astrology and psychic hotlines, let me tell you why it offends God. He would like to have a relationship with you. He is your Daddy and deserves all of your love and attention. Why look to the stars, which He made, or other people, whom He created, when He wants to communicate with you directly? He does not want you running around with other lovers, whether they be demon-inspired psychics on the other end of the phone, ungodly friends or anyone else who gives you people-centered advice about your life.

Only God is the true interpreter of the dreams, visions and events that make up our life. Only He can offer genuine insight into the purpose of those valleys we walked through. Don't look to the stars—look to the Star!

So, Joseph gave the cupbearer the interpretation of his dream, indicating that he would be restored to his old position in three days. The baker liked what he heard, so he asked for an interpretation of his dream, but his was less favorable. He would die in three days. Not good, but the truth.

Then Joseph asked the cupbearer for a favor: "Do you think, when you get out of here, that you could mention me to someone?" Look how he describes his situation:

> For I was forcibly carried off from the land of the Hebrews, and even here I have done nothing to deserve being put in a dungeon.
>
> —Genesis 40:15

Did he tell the truth? Yes. Did he point fingers and play the blame game? Not a bit. There is not a hint of bitterness in that statement. He did not go into the gory details of how badly he was hurt and what he was doing to recover. He simply asked for help.

I cannot count the times I have a conversation with someone, and they spend most of their time singing the "Somebody Done Me Wrong" song. It is always someone else's fault.

Joseph could have whined and complained, "My lame brothers backstabbed me. They wanted to kill me, but I narrowly escaped. Then they sold me into slavery. Then I was doing really well for Potiphar, but his stupid rich wife had this thing for me, and I wouldn't touch her, so she makes up this sexual harassment story..." Joseph could have whined away his days in jail singing sad but true tales of how badly and unfairly life had treated him. I am sure it would have been a hit with his jail mates. But if he had, he would have never been released, and if you do, you will never find your way out of the valley of resentment and bitterness.

Your problem will always be a problem if you are still blaming somebody. It is impossible for opportunity to grow in the soil of resentment. You will never break free of the shackles of a wrong perspective until you let go of the details and say, "You know what? I was treated unfairly. Now I'm going to leave that behind and do the best I can right where I am."

ELLEN'S STORY

Within hours of her birth, Ellen's mother left her on a park bench, wrapped in a blanket. A policeman found her and brought her to an orphanage. At six months of age, she was placed in a foster home, where she was abused, then sent back to the orphanage.

Hundreds of miles away a young American couple decided to adopt a child after losing their unborn baby. The adoption agency told them of a baby who had exceptional needs.

"This baby can't hold up her head. She can't sit up. She can't move. She just lies there. You are not going to have a normal child," the adoption officer told them. They adopted Ellen anyway.

When Ellen was two years old, her adoptive parents

divorced, and her mother raised her. As Ellen grew up, she began to put up walls and barriers to real relationships. She began to believe that if anyone knew the real Ellen, they would reject her as her birth mother had.

Ellen came to know the Lord, but she had a hard time relating to Him as a father because she had never really known a father. In high school she dated a lot, and her insecurities led her into unhealthy relationships. When she graduated, she felt the Lord giving her a choice to either follow Him or live life by her own choices.

She chose to serve God and decided to attend Bible college. There she learned to rely on the Lord wholeheartedly, not allowing her past to define her. She also began attending church. Because she didn't have a car, a young man from the college ministry offered to give her a ride every week. Romance blossomed, and three years later they were married.

Ellen had to overcome some big obstacles to be where she is now. For years she swore she would never marry and have children. Today, she devotes her life to her husband and children, and she finds her fulfillment in them.

She went from being abandoned on a park bench to being the wife and mom of a terrific family.

Ellen did not let her problems define her life. Like Joseph, against all odds she kept her dream alive.

No matter what you have been hit with, what you face, what you have gone through or are going through, God says that you are going to make it.

Rather than cursing or rehearsing our scars, we need to see them as emblems of God's grace. We need to see our problems as opportunities.

You may have scars on the outside or inside, but you are still alive. God has you here for a reason. Remember my wife's burned hand and the lingering fear of fire? God soon healed that as well. All that remains now are slight physical scars, reminders of God's grace to my wife and me. And that baby she was pregnant with? He now serves on staff at our church, and he and his wife have made us proud grandparents.

No one can promise you that all those scars will disappear. But rather than letting them destroy you, let them remind you of the mess you came out of and the message you have now. Let them remind you of the tombstone that became your steppingstone.

Chapter 8

Miracles Can Happen As Suddenly As Tragedies

The young man working in the Iowa grocery store didn't seem like much. He had dreams, but they never seemed to culminate in anything. He would stock shelves at night, talking about the day he would become a full-time quarterback for a football team.

He had been talking like that for years, but his sports career had been disappointing. Out of high school he had received no scholarship offers from Division 1-A schools. He only started as quarterback during his fifth year in college, and no professional team drafted him.

He tried out for a National Football League team, but was cut. He played for three years with a lesser-known league, keeping his family afloat financially by working at the grocery store.

When the NFL finally showed interest, they sent him to one of their European teams. He was passed over in an expansion draft, but was later signed to play in St. Louis as backup to the starting quarterback in December 1997.

He saw his first career action a year later when the starting quarterback was injured, giving the backup the chance he had dreamed of. And then on January 30, 2000, he led his team to victory in Super Bowl XXXIV, winning the Super Bowl Most Valuable Player award and dazzling critics who when the season began barely knew his name—Kurt Warner.[1]

Warner went from being a no-name commodity to having one of the most outstanding seasons the NFL has ever seen. By the way, Warner is a Bible-believing Christian who gives God glory every chance he gets.

What is the fuel that gives us the energy to bounce back time and again and see problems as opportunities? Faith. Or more accurately, faith in God. Warner had a stubborn faith that he was on the right path and that God would make sense of his life.

It is fashionable these days to talk about "faith" and "trust" apart from God, as if faith and trust needed no object. If you turn on certain daytime talk shows, you hear people speaking in quasi-spiritual terms about how "faith" helped them through a problem. However, unless our faith is firmly in God, it goes nowhere.

I had an acquaintance in high school who, under the influence of drugs, believed that he was indestructible. So strong was his "faith" that he drove his motorcycle headfirst into a truck. He had great faith that he was indestructible, but that faith proved to be wrongly placed. If faith were all he needed, he would still be alive today.

One of the most-quoted chapters in the Bible is Hebrews 11, and for good reason. Its synopsis of faith in the lives of Old Testament heroes gives us a hint at how important faith is in God's eyes.

The faith factor determines how high you will bounce.

Now faith is the substance of things hoped for, the evidence of things not seen.

—HEBREWS 11:1, KJV

How do we see a solution in our problem? Faith. How do we know God is going to straighten out that business fiasco? Faith. How do we know God is going to heal our bodies? Faith.

Faith in God. Nothing more.

Recently a major network aired a controversial show called *Magic Secrets Revealed*. I have been to magic shows, and even though I know in my head it is not real, it is astonishing how they make huge things like cars and elephants disappear, how they chop people in half and make people float through rings.

After watching the network show, much of the amazement is gone. It really is smoke and mirrors, contortions and sleight of hand.

Faith is not a magic trick. It is not pretending something to be true when we know it is not. Faith is real, through and through. In fact, it is more real than what we see with our eyes. The Bible says that heaven and earth will pass away, but God's Word will never pass away. So faith is substance. It is the anchor of our soul that keeps us steady in turbulent, stormy waters.

It is nice when our faith is clothed—when there is some evidence to back us up, something that satisfies our logic. Sometimes natural circumstances, or supernatural signs and wonders, support our faith. At other times no evidence is to be found. All we have is the promise of God. We have absolutely nothing to go on but an undying faith in what God said. I like to call that "naked faith"—faith that is based solely on the Word of God.

Notice that the writer of Hebrews compares faith to evidence. Evidence can determine whether someone is guilty or innocent, liable or not at fault, incarcerated or free to go.

The Greek word for *evidence* in this passage is the same word that was used for a title deed. A deed proves that a house or car is ours, and sometimes that's all the proof we have. In the face of attack and criticism, when we don't feel saved, healed, blessed or delivered, faith is the pink slip that assures us we are. So the next time the devil asks you where your promised blessing is, show him the title deed—your faith.

Faith is the fuel that keeps your hopes and dreams from running out of gas.

THE LORD IS WITH YOU

Despite his promise to help Joseph once he was released from prison, the Bible simply notes, "The chief cupbearer, however, did not remember Joseph; he forgot him" (Gen. 40:23). Sometimes those we help the most do not return the favor. To depend upon other people for help in our own time of trouble is a recipe for disaster.

Thankfully, Joseph had someone who had not forgotten him. Genesis 39:23 says that "the LORD was with Joseph and gave him success in whatever he did."

I wonder if Joseph knew that at the time. Did he feel God close by, or was there an inner chill? I wonder if serving time in jail felt like the kind of success he had been dreaming of for years. No evidence existed that he was on the right track. His faith must have been naked.

We don't know, but I have to believe that at some point during those thirteen years of slavery and imprisonment, Joseph went through days, or weeks, or months of silence from God. Everything, including his family, friends, dignity and respect, had been taken from him.

The only thing that could not be taken from Joseph was his faith in God. Faith knows that no matter how deep your valley is, no matter how long it has been since you have heard from Him, Jesus has never left your side. I remember a children's song that tells us that because the world didn't give us His love, it cannot take it away.

Joseph could have wiled away his time in prison bemoaning his unjust conviction. Not only had he served Potiphar faithfully, but he had also been the source of his master's prosperity. Potiphar had initially put Joseph in charge of certain areas of his household. From the moment he had, the Lord blessed everything Potiphar possessed, both in the house and in the field. Joseph was so full of integrity, so clearly under the Lord's hand of blessing, that Potiphar finally said, "Here is the checkbook. Here are the credit cards. You pay the bills. You decide what needs to be ordered. You are in charge." For his part, Potiphar was able to kick back, relax and enjoy his money.

It looked on the surface that being sold into slavery in Egypt may have been a blessing in disguise. Now, sitting in jail, victimized, betrayed and forgotten, Joseph wasn't so sure. Prison gives a man time to think—time to consider what he could have done to avoid his life in chains.

If only he had not had the misfortune of coming into contact with Potiphar's wife. It wasn't his fault he was young and attractive, and she a rich, bored socialite with a penchant for lying.

Perhaps while eating prison food Joseph thought, *I still believe I did the right thing. I could never have slept with her. I have too much respect for myself, and besides, my boss—her husband—didn't deserve to have the trust he placed in me so abused. I just wish he would have believed me. That wife of his is some liar. But then again, I am only a slave. Who is going to believe a slave? Now, things have gone from bad to worse.*

All of us are tempted to feel sorry for ourselves and play

145

the well-deserved victim role. Joseph, however, refused to succumb to that temptation. He had come too far to quit now. Joseph knew who he was. He knew his position, but he also knew his limits. One of the hallmarks of faith is keeping our words and deeds in line with God's Word—no matter what situation or invitation we encounter. He had been tempted sexually, but he had stayed pure. Now he was being tempted to feel sorry for himself and give up on the promises of God. He would keep the faith.

Do you know who you are?

More importantly, do you know who God is?

He is a God who rewards integrity, who rewards faith in Him.

Joseph knew that. He would not sell out his destiny for a night with anyone.

As a student in college I had the great privilege of hearing Billy Graham address a gathering of aspiring ministers. Looking directly at us, he warned, "Young men, three things destroy ministry and sometimes ministers—pride, sex and money." He proceeded to give vivid and even humorous examples of all three of those things in his life.

The story he told concerning sexual temptation has always reminded me of Joseph and Potiphar's wife. He told of an associate who was with him during a crusade in Paris. Graham's staff had been put up in a first-class hotel, but it was in the middle of a rather upscale red light district.

This associate became so tempted during the night that he literally locked himself in his room—something you can do with European doors—and threw the key out the window so that he could not get out that night. The next morning he had to call housekeeping to let him out of his own room.

Then Billy Graham told us, "I made a decision years ago that I would never, ever, for any reason be alone with any woman except my wife, both to protect me from accusations and to protect me from anything unwanted happening."

Graham set himself up to succeed. Joseph had too by fleeing the advances of Potiphar's wife. He literally did what Paul told Timothy to do: "Flee also youthful lusts" (2 Tim. 2:22, KJV).

Like sin, Potiphar's wife had been relentless. As a Christian, you will not be tested once and then left alone; you will be tested again and again. And, like the devil, when she could not get what she wanted, Potiphar's wife instantly changed character. The same hand that had been seductively beckoning Joseph now turned an accusing finger toward him. The same mouth that had called him "lover" and "handsome" now cursed him. In Genesis 39:17, she called him "that Hebrew."

That Hebrew was a derogatory, racist term. Joseph hadn't just been up against a wicked woman, but against the power system of Egypt that thought Hebrews were inferior. It would have been like a white woman accusing a black slave on her plantation in the 1800s.

Now it all seemed like a bad dream. Except every day Joseph awoke to a very real prison. Joseph had no evidence that God was with him. He didn't need any—he had a naked faith in God and in his dreams. Again, sometimes the only way we learn that God is all we need is when God is all we have.

"DA MAN"

What do we do when we have nothing left? When we are in prison? Broke? Without a friend? Those are the times when raw faith kicks in.

Some things in life seem to take forever to happen, but once they do, they make your head spin with their swiftness. Whether it is a tragedy or a miracle, in an instant life can change dramatically.

147

I will never forget when Marguerite was pregnant with our first child. We did not know if it was a boy or girl. We didn't care; we were enormously excited to be parents. Those nine months were so long. We decorated the room...and waited. We thought of names...and waited. We bought a stroller and a crib...and waited.

We bought a lamp for the baby's room, and on it were a figurine and a music box. I remember the little song it used to play. For weeks before the baby finally came, I would sing with the music box, "Come out, Baby, come out."

Twenty-some years later, I am shocked when I look back and realize how quickly the baby came, grew up and moved out. Somebody put him into turbo speed! I have two other kids in college. I thought it would never happen. Now I wonder, "What happened?"

More recently, I found myself unable to wait to be a grandparent. That first baby I could not wait to have announced to my wife and me, "You're going to be grandparents." Though it seems impossible, I'm a grandpa. And I know that one day I am going to wake up and be eighty years old, the grandkids will have grown up and moved out, and I am going to say, "What happened? Now I've got more grandkids than I can count, and the great-grandkids are running circles around me."

Waiting is hard enough when you know the length of time—nine months for a baby, twenty-three days until Christmas, three more weeks before vacation. Waiting seems excruciating when you have no idea how long it is going to take. Can you imagine how Joseph felt in prison? He had no idea if he would ever get out. No use marking off the days and weeks, for this meant nothing if no end were in sight.

Through it all, Joseph never stopped trusting God. Then suddenly, out of the blue and without warning, his day of deliverance came. One day he woke up in shackles and went to sleep wearing Pharoah's signet ring.

He went from being inmate #1739548, a forgotten "victim," to being "da man" in Egypt—all in one day. Miracles can happen as suddenly as tragedies.

Pharaoh had a dream. In it he saw seven fat and beautiful cows come out of the Nile River. Then Pharaoh saw seven scrawny, ugly cows come out, and they ate the seven fat, beautiful cows.

That wasn't all. He had another dream of seven beautiful ears of corn. Then seven other ears of corn grew up skinny and ugly, and they ate the beautiful ears.

Pharaoh was disturbed; he knew the dreams had meaning. These weren't random, too-much-pizza nightmares; there was a germ of reality in them. So he called his in-house psychic hotline—the best astrologers in Egypt—but they could not interpret the dreams. God had blinded their eyes, and they knew they could not just throw out some user-friendly, textbook answer. They had to give a real interpretation, or Pharaoh could have them executed.

So they said, "We don't know. Go ask someone else. The connection's not good this morning, Your Majesty. The tarot cards aren't working."

Then the cupbearer, after forgetting Joseph for two years, remembered, and Joseph was summoned.

His miracle was about to strike with the same suddenness as his tragedies.

THE APPOINTED TIME

You have heard it before: Delay is not denial. In Psalm 105:18–19, the psalmist says of Joseph:

> They bruised his feet with shackles, his neck was put in irons, till what he foretold came to pass, till the word of the LORD proved him true.

God had an appointed time for Joseph's deliverance. Until that time came, God was seeing if Joseph would keep the faith and hang on to the dream. God was busy working to make everything turn out right at precisely the right moment—in His time. He was working on Pharaoh, working on Egypt, working on Joseph, getting all of the details to work in harmony for His glory.

The answer to your prayer may involve people, places and things of which you are totally unaware. You may be praying for your dad's salvation and rather impatiently be wondering why it is taking so long. God sees all the strings that are attached to the answer. He is doing all the advance work so it turns out good for everybody, not just for you and your dad. In the meantime, He is using that delay to build character in you to see if you can keep your dream alive in the midst of a prison-confined experience.

I love the declaration of faith Joseph makes when he first sees Pharaoh face to face:

> "I cannot do it," Joseph replied to Pharoah, "but God will give Pharaoh the answer he desires."
>
> —GENESIS 41:16

Only God can give the true interpretation, not ungodly friends, psychic hotlines or mind-readers. Joseph interprets Pharoah's dreams, both of which point to the same calamity: Seven years of famine will come to Egypt after seven years of bounty.

Remember that in those days famine did not simply mean food lines or a downturn in the economy. Famine meant death. Though it sounds gross, famine could even result in cannibalism. Famine meant extreme desperation.

Joseph not only saw the famine coming, but he also stepped up with a plan. No one else even knew what the dreams meant, but Joseph had a handle on both the dream and what to do about it. A man with a dream and a plan is unstoppable.

There is an old saying: "Luck is when hard work meets opportunity." Whether as a slave or a prisoner, Joseph had both worked hard and kept the faith. He had refused to give up. He said no to bitterness and despair. Thus, when the opportunity finally came, he was a man with a dream and a plan.

He told Pharaoh, "What you ought to do during these seven years of abundance is build great big barns and sheds where you can store grain. Don't eat all of it. Store a portion of it, so that when the seven years of famine hit, you will have something to eat."

Pharaoh said, "Joseph, I like it. I hereby put you in charge of Egypt."

That's like Bill Gates telling you, "I like your plan. I want you to run Microsoft. I'll still be the top guy, but practically speaking, you're in charge of everything." Mr. Gates then gives you his corporate credit card, his Mercedes Benz, a wardrobe of Versace suits, alligator skin shoes and Wolfgang Puck as your personal chef.

Joseph's faith collided with a major impending disaster, and in one of the most dazzling single moments in the entire Bible, God elevated him from the dungeon to the royal palace and set in motion a plan to save the lives of countless thousands. Joseph woke up in prison, but he went to sleep in a palace. So can you if you keep the faith.

Oh, one more thing. As icing on the cake, not only was Joseph free, but he was also showered with honor and praise.

> He [Pharaoh] had him [Joseph] ride in a chariot as his second-in-command, and men shouted before him, "Make way."
>
> —GENESIS 41:43

Some translations prefer "bow down." Joseph got to zip around the city with guys running ahead of him saying, in modern terms, "Out of the way! Here comes da man!"

THE MIRACLE WILL COME

Some of you have been through the tragedy, and you are still waiting for the dream. You carry the scars, but you wonder what they are for. You have passed the test and been through the mess, but where is the testimony and the message? You have been hit and have bounced back, yet you still wonder when, and perhaps if, God is going to use you.

Don't give up now! Who knows what tomorrow will bring? Your dream may be twenty-four hours away from fulfillment. And if you have gone through the test of faith and held fast, one day God is going to spring a surprise deliverance on you, and it will make your head spin. You will probably be asking for more time to get ready.

Chuck Burr, a member of the 1964 Buffalo Bills team that won the American Football League championship, lost his championship ring six years after the Bills won the championship. Burr was playing catch on a beach in Ontario, Canada, and his championship ring flew off his finger and disappeared into the water and sand. Crushed, Burr scoured the beach for the ring, but to no avail.

Thirty years later, a beachcomber with a metal detector found the ring, which is engraved with Burr's name. Burr, then 77, was ecstatic. Clearly, he never thought he would see it again.[2]

Some of us feel the same way. It has been decades since our devastating loss or tragic event, but God has not forgotten us. He is preparing us for the day of restoration, and with Him, we will always find those things that have been lost.

On one hand, it seems that the future will never arrive.

Waiting is difficult. On the other hand, the future arrives before we are ready for it. It is like the Second Coming of Christ. Sometimes even strong believers can begin to wonder if it is ever going to happen. However, once the events start to unravel, there will not be time for scholars and TV evangelists to talk about it. Despite God's patience, many will still complain that they were not ready—it just happened too fast.

God gives us time to think about what He has for us. He takes us through valleys not only to refine us, but also to allow us to ponder what is ahead.

Are you ready for God to spring a sudden miracle on your life? You may be spiritually dressed in jail clothes and shackles and addicted to frustration, stress, drugs, hatred and unhappiness—but God is about to work it out. He sees your faith and is getting ready to elevate you. He is getting ready to breathe on those old bones, causing your dead dreams and dashed hopes to spring to life.

He is going to put His signet ring on your finger, a gold chain around your neck and send angels in front of you to say, "Out of the way! Here comes da man!"

DO-NOTHING DREAMS

Joseph was now in charge. The last verse of Genesis 41 says, "All the countries came to Egypt to buy grain from Joseph" (v. 57). I am guessing he became enormously wealthy and made Egypt wealthy as well. He blessed others, and God blessed him.

Meanwhile, back at the ranch, Jacob and his eleven remaining sons were trying to live through the famine in the land of Canaan. Jacob was a wealthy man, though still grieved over the loss of Joseph. Despite his wealth, the famine was beginning to have its affect. He had learned that there was grain in Egypt, so at least there was hope.

But nobody in his family was taking action.

Finally he turned to his sons, who had run out of ideas, and said to them, "Why do you just keep looking at each other?" (Gen. 42:1).

What a great question—one I would like to ask a lot of people today. Most people have desires. That is to say, they would like to be rich and famous, or powerful and influential. Maybe their aspirations are more modest—a good business, a loving family and a healthy body. They call their desire a dream. Yet they sit around doing nothing. Thus, they have a "do-nothing" marriage, a "do-nothing" job and a "do-nothing" church life. They are going no place fast, and still they sit around waiting for something to happen. Nothing ever does.

Jacob's sons were no different, sitting around staring at the walls while their stomachs growled. They remind me of the lepers in Israel during the time that Syria put a siege on Samaria. They sat outside the gate of the city because they were unclean, but they still heard the terrible news that things inside the city walls had deteriorated to the point where people were starting to eat each other. They had had enough. Finally they said to each other, "Why sit here till we die? Let's go to the Syrian camp. At least they have food."

"They'll kill us," one said. "Not only are we the enemy, but we're lepers—a double whammy!"

"You're probably right," another responded. "It is a one in a million chance that we will survive. But think about it— sitting here doing nothing gives us a 0 percent chance of living." (See 2 Kings 7:3–4.)

To me, one of the most frustrating things about the ministry is preaching to people week after week, month after month and year after year who simply sit, soak and sour. They have atomic bomb potential, but for whatever reason they have settled for firecracker lives. Their marriage may be on the rocks, but they will not attend a marriage seminar. Their drinking problem is relentless, but they will not attend our twelve-step program. Their kids are wigging out, but they will not take them to the youth group. "That won't work," they reason. And they might be right. But what they are doing now is definitely not working. More often than not, they are actually not doing anything.

Do we still expect the old approach to work?

There is an old joke about a guy who came to work every day complaining about lunch.

"Bologna sandwich again! I hate bologna!"

His coworkers heard this for so long that finally one of them said, "If you don't like bologna sandwiches, tell your wife not to make them."

He said, "My wife doesn't make my lunch. I do."

The point: If you do what you have always done, you are going to get what you have always had. Some day God may look at you and say, "How long are you going to sit there with the same old solutions, which aren't solutions at all? Get up and go! The answer will never be found in the sitting, but in the going."

Jacob challenged his sons, "Why don't you guys go to Egypt? It may be risky, but it's better than waiting here to die."

Ten of them went, but Jacob would not let Benjamin go.

It had been twenty years since the brothers had seen Joseph, and he had probably changed quite a bit. When they arrived, they did not recognize him, but Joseph recognized them.

Imagine how Joseph's heart must have beat when he saw out of the corner of his eye the familiar frame of Judah, the face of Reuben and the recognizable step of his other brothers. How the memories must have flooded back!

Unrecognized, Joseph stepped forward and, with a little

trickery of his own, accused them of being spies. This may seem cruel, but Joseph knew his brothers. He may not have believed they were spies, but he knew they didn't have spotless character. He wanted to see what kind of men they had become after all these years.

And where was Benjamin? Did they get rid of him, too? Joseph needed a way to find out without disclosing his identity, so he fabricated this test.

Despite their protests of innocence, assuring the ruler that they were only there to buy grain, Joseph refused to relent. This time he had the power. He told them to prove their story by going home and returning with Benjamin. Oh, and for collateral, they would leave Simeon in Egypt.

When the brothers heard this, they were nervous and scared. Their minds immediately went to their sin from years ago.

> Surely we are being punished because of our brother. We saw how distressed he was when he pleaded with us for his life, but we would not listen.
>
> —GENESIS 42:21

Guilt turns normal people into paranoiacs. When you are having an affair, every phone call makes you jump. When you are crooked in your business, you cannot look anyone in the eye. When you are a criminal and someone is nice to you, you suspect they have bad intentions. Joseph's brothers were sure they were now being repaid for the sin they had committed years ago.

When they returned home to their father, without yet another of his sons, the pain of the past welled up in Jacob. He was still haunted by the hurt of losing Joseph. Jacob had never completely left that valley; he had not let the wound heal, and as a result, he was prone to self-pity. Jacob wailed:

> You have deprived me of my children. Joseph is no
> more and Simeon is no more, and now you want to take
> Benjamin. Everything is against me!
>
> —GENESIS 42:36

When we see things through the lens of past hurts, we are
blind to approaching miracles. Little did Jacob know that his
tragedy was about to take a hard U-turn; his miracle was
alive and waiting for him in Egypt.

Jacob's problem was not his problem. If he had seen
reality as God did, he would have known that his problems
and impossibilities were God's solutions and miracles.
Jacob's problem was how he saw the problem.

Jacob refused to send Benjamin until the famine wors-
ened. Judah finally volunteered to be Benjamin's personal
bodyguard, pledging to keep him alive at all costs. Jacob
became resigned and said, "If I have to go down to my grave
grieving, then so be it, because we are going to die if things
don't change." God was allowing the heat of circumstance to
change "do-nothings" into men of action and faith. Sure,
there was still risk—faith always involves risk—but the risk
of doing nothing was greater.

They went back to Egypt with more money and some
unique gifts from Jacob to appease Pharaoh. There, Joseph
tested them one more time by putting his personal goblet in
Benjamin's sack and claiming he stole it.

I think he was seeing what his brothers were made of.
Were they the same guys who ate and drank while Joseph
screamed for his life in the cistern? Were they still heart-
less? Cold? If so, they would leave Benjamin to serve as a
slave and save their own skin.

They didn't. They began to intercede for Benjamin. Judah,
with courage having replaced immaturity, stepped up and
said, "Keep me. I will serve as a slave in his place. Benjamin

would not have done something like this. My father has already lost one son. He doesn't want to go to his grave having lost another."

> Then Joseph could not longer control himself before all his attendants, and he cried out, "Have everyone leave my presence!" So there was no one with Joseph when he made himself known to his brothers. And he wept so loudly that the Egyptians heard him, and Pharaoh's household heard about it.
>
> Joseph said to his brothers, "I am Joseph! Is my father still living?" But his brothers were not able to answer him, because they were terrified at his presence.
>
> Then Joseph said to his brothers, "Come close to me." When they had done so, he said, "I am your brother Joseph, the one you sold into Egypt! And now, do not be distressed and do not be angry with yourselves for selling me here, because it was to save lives that God sent me ahead of you."
>
> GENESIS 45:1–5

Seventeen years later, after Jacob died, Joseph repeated this to his brothers when they started wondering if he was finally going to pay them back.

> You intended to harm me, but God intended it for good to accomplish what is now being done, the saving of many lives.
>
> —GENESIS 50:20

Anyone who has ever been hurt, abused or used ought to take a close look at this verse. Every Christian ought to know this verse by heart. It speaks to the very core of our hurts and to the very lowest place in our valley. No matter how life has treated us, how we have hurt ourselves with sin or how others have hurt us, God intends to accomplish something great with it—if, like Joseph, we let go of bitterness and allow Him to turn our sorrow into joy, our weakness into strength and our tragedies into triumph.

How long will you allow the enemy to keep you in that pit of despair, chained by hopelessness and bound by bitterness? Sometimes we need to get angry about what is going on in our lives. Remember the old movie *Network?* Peter Finch was the actor, and he had the famous line, "I'm mad as hell, and I'm not going to take it anymore!"

The language may be offensive to some Christian ears, but at times we ought to share the sentiment. Are you mad enough about what the enemy has stolen that you are not going to take it anymore? Are you ready for God to turn it around?

This is not simply a matter of "when life gives you lemons, make lemonade." This is a matter of letting God heal your hurts and then allowing Him to redeem your past by using it to build you and bless others. What was meant for your harm God can use to touch the lives of others.

Joseph wasn't focused on his past; he was focused on the present and the future. Past hurts neither tied him down with bitterness nor drove him to seek revenge. He simply recognized how God was using all of it, wasting none of it, to create a better today and more hopeful tomorrow. Paul says in Philippians:

> But one thing I do: forgetting what is behind and straining toward what is ahead, I press on...
>
> —PHILIPPIANS 3:13–14

I remember the movie *City Slickers* with Jack Palance as Curly, and he kept holding up his index finger signifying "one thing." The whole movie they wondered what that one thing was. It ended up meaning that he had simplified his life to the most important thing, and he left the rest behind.

That's how we should be. Leaving the junk behind, not playing the blame game, we press on, straining to see what God has next for us, knowing that in all things He is at work to make our lives a symphony of grace.

✦

Section III
Drop Your Burdens, Pick Up Your Credentials

Chapter 9

God Has a Purpose

It is difficult to see purpose in our problems, especially when we are in the middle of them. Still, while we often cannot see the whys or wherefores, God is weaving our life experiences into a beautiful work of art, not wasting a thread. Once we see His handiwork, we cannot help but marvel.

I remember hearing about a family camp in the 1970s attended by a young woman who had been a member of a motorcycle gang. She had been saved for a year or so and was doing pretty well, but she had one time run over and killed a two-year-old boy by accident. The thought of the incident haunted her. Even though she was saved, she was still in bondage to the pain and shame.

The teacher at the camp had become a Spirit-filled Christian in the early days of the Charismatic movement. He was speaking that week about how Jesus heals our past, present and future. His teaching was helping her to move beyond her own past.

During the service on the last night, a rather unusual thing happened. During the middle of the service, a couple jumped up and ran out of the room, obviously in distress. A few of the ushers wisely followed them into the foyer and tried to comfort them, but to no avail. This young woman felt a prompting in her spirit to go talk with them, and she got up from her seat and went to the foyer.

She arrived just in time to hear the man say to the ushers, "But you don't understand. You just don't understand. You see, I've killed a man, and you just don't know what that's like."

In the timing of the Lord, she stepped forward and said, "I know what that's like. I met Jesus there, and you can, too."

THE SAME COMFORT

Some of us have disqualified ourselves from ever being useful to God again because of the pain we have been through. Others are overwhelmed by the shame of their own sin and failures. But God wants to use us as He used that young woman that night to speak healing into the lives of other people.

There are couples in our church who went through the pain of divorce, not to mention the shame of not making it as a Christian couple. While others rejected them, God helped them recover—and some are now being used to help other married couples. There are former drug addicts helping current drug addicts, and former adulterers are helping to keep people from adultery or to recover from the shame of having failed. Name your sin—there are people in churches and ministries around the world who are ministering out of their own life experiences.

There is a woman in our congregation named Hope who went through a divorce and has allowed God to use her experience. "No one can really describe the pain of divorce," she wrote me recently. "I grew up in a Christian home with my parents' marriage as a model. There was never any doubt in my mind that I would marry someone and carry on the tradition of a solid home. I went into ministry and met the man I believed God had prepared for me. We had two children and what I believed was a good marriage. We also continued in the ministry.

"After more than twenty years of marriage, my husband went into a classic midlife crisis. I tried to be patient with him, but our marriage continued to disintegrate. I was sure we could work things out. Divorce was not an option for the two of us, or so I thought. Two years later he walked out and wanted nothing more to do with our marriage."

Hope depended on the Lord as her "husband." Recently she has felt Him leading her to minister from her hurt.

"God began to give me ideas of how He would use my pain for His kingdom," she wrote. "Having been a women's conference speaker in the past, I began to develop a new series on how God is a husband. He has also given me a desire to put together a curriculum for single moms and their kids. I can envision how God can use me to help single moms and their kids pick up the pieces of their lives and see God in a new way. There is life after devastation, and I now thank God for choosing me to share this message with others."

It is time to drop our burdens and pick up our credentials. God never wastes a hurt. Paul gives us a clue as to why God allows us to go through some of the things we go through.

> Praise be to the God and Father of our Lord Jesus Christ, the Father of compassion and the God of all comfort, who comforts us in all our troubles, so that we can comfort those in any trouble with the comfort we ourselves have received from God.
>
> —2 CORINTHIANS 1:3–4

At least in part, this answers the question, "Why do we have to go through all this mess?" God does not want to heal us merely for our own benefit; His desire is that the same comfort we received during our season of hardship can become the platform from which we minister to someone who is going through their own valley. Rather than our hurts breaking us, as the enemy intended, God has redeemed them to the point where others are being helped and encouraged. By the time God is finished with us, the enemy will be sorry he ever brought catastrophe on us.

Paul goes on to say in 2 Corinthians 4:1:

> Therefore, since through God's mercy we have this ministry, we do not lose heart.

Isn't it interesting that ministry often comes as a result of God's mercy? And often the very areas where we had hurt the most, the areas where there was the deepest pain, become the areas God turns into our platform to speak into other people's lives.

Again, Paul writes:

> And we know that in all things God works together for the good of those who love him, who have been called according to his purpose.
>
> —ROMANS 8:28

Notice that the verse does not guarantee that all things will work together for everybody's good. This is not a promise to every person who has ever been born, but to those who love God and are called according to His purpose.

If you love God, this promise is yours.

If you do not love God, then sadly, your hurts may well be wasted.

I sometimes read biographies of famous people or watch

them on television. Particularly sad are the biographies of great leaders or popular celebrities who experienced great success, only eventually to find themselves spiraling downward until they die of drug overdoses or drinking-related problems. Their talents were many and their prospects bright, but they could not escape life's hurts any more than you or I can.

Those are wasted hurts. They never gave God a chance to redeem the pain.

The difference between you and the world is not that you have been spared life's worst hits, but that God will use those hits to help His kingdom—if you let Him.

KEVIN AND SUSAN

Kevin's father was a violent alcoholic. Once when Kevin was a teenager, he saw his father stepping off a curb in a drunken stupor. A plan flashed through his mind: He would run him over, ending the pain he, his mother and his siblings had been put through. Kevin stepped on the gas and sped toward his father, but when he got close to him, he slammed on the brakes, sending the car sideways and hitting his father with the bumper. His father looked at him with glazed eyes, never knowing exactly what had happened or how close he came to dying.

It is hardly a surprise, then, that Kevin didn't know how to be a good husband or father when he married. He married his sweetheart, Susan, but young love went sour early on. When he returned from a tour of duty in Southeast Asia, she had decided she no longer needed him. She hated the moment he was to return and resented him for not being there to help raise the children. She calculated that she could earn enough on her income to support her burgeoning family, so she told Kevin that she did not love him and asked him to leave.

It didn't come as too harsh of a blow to him. He was in love with the things of the world, and he figured a divorce would give him freedom to enjoy the good life. But one day he was driving home and saw a church located in a shopping center. The church building had once been a supermarket. Even though he was offended that a church would be located in such a place—in his mind, churches had steeples and stained-glass windows—something drew him in, and he asked to speak with the pastor. While he waited, his life began to unfold before his eyes like a film reel. He remembered his father, his family, his tour in Southeast Asia—all the things that had made him who he was. Overwhelmed, he got up to leave, but one of the pastors at Faith Community stopped him and said, "I can see that you are hurting. Jesus loves you, and He can help you."

Kevin accepted Christ that afternoon, a decision that would change his life, but Susan was not so easily convinced. He went home and said, "Guess what? I became a Christian today."

She looked at him and said, "So what? Do you think after more than ten years of making my life miserable things are going to change just because you tell me you got religion?"

But things did change. And after much persuasion, Susan finally agreed to join Kevin at church. The Lord touched her heart, and though she didn't respond to the altar call, she gave her life to Christ right where she sat.

As a couple, they began to experience true peace and fulfillment. Their lives radically changed. They could not get enough of the Word, and they started attending different Bible studies at the church. Susan joined the women's ministries. Both sensed that God was healing them from the pain in their backgrounds.

After a honeymoon period with the Lord, the next few

years were difficult. Kevin and Susan had to work hard to rebuild a relationship with each other. Many of the trust issues and old arguments continued to plague them, but the Lord was faithful in bringing them through.

Now, Kevin and Susan are leaders in the altar ministry at our church. In addition, they are involved in counseling other couples; they graciously make themselves available to receive calls from couples who are in trouble and need to talk to somebody. Kevin and Susan are open about sharing their testimony. Their story encourages couples that, although their marriage is in the ashes, God is able to resurrect it.

I have heard Kevin and Susan say on numerous occasions, "We tell other couples, 'God can help you. We know it. We have been through it.' They get hope from that. If He could do it for two people who hated each other, He certainly can do the same for them. And He does. He is no respecter of persons."

Kevin and Susan not only recovered from the pain of their past and the threat of divorce, but they made a decision to drop their burdens and pick up their credentials. Rather than destroying them, God used their past to qualify them for fruitful ministry. Sure, it meant leaving a lot of garbage behind, but they are survivors. Actually, they are more than survivors. Like Joseph, what was meant for harm is now being used to minister to others.

"FAT AND UGLY"

There is a precious young lady in our church named Stephanie who has been overweight virtually all her life. She began dieting in elementary school, going on popular weight-loss programs or taking advice from doctors, but each time she failed. As a result, Stephanie was belittled by her family and friends, particularly her grandfather who told her she was fat and ugly, that she would never find a husband or get a job.

While in high school, she grew tired of being overweight and crying herself to sleep every night, so she decided not to eat for one whole day. She lost so much weight that she decided to do it again. Eventually, her goal became to weigh less than one hundred pounds, and she was willing to do anything to get there—even if it meant risking her life.

She relapsed the following week and went on an eating binge. Overcome with guilt, she forced herself to throw up, beginning a pattern of bulimic behavior that lasted six years. But instead of losing weight, she would go through periods of compulsive overeating that caused her to gain more pounds.

Finally, she came to church and found Christ, and she began a road to recovery. During her last semester of college, she did a study of eating disorders and proposed a theory based on Christian principles. During that time, the Lord led her to a woman who was caught in the stranglehold of anorexia and bulimia, and Stephanie helped this woman toward recovery. God is in the process of transforming her secret shame into public ministry that has the potential to help hundreds, perhaps thousands.

WOUNDS BECOME WINDOWS

Do you see the pattern? God never wastes a hurt. As they heal, our wounds become windows, and we see God's purpose more clearly. We see His plan for our life, and His desire to help others through us.

A woman wrote me recently to share her experience. For several years of her childhood, she was molested by a neighbor. She had her first thoughts of suicide in elementary school, and actually attempted suicide when her father left the family during her early teen years. After that, she gave her heart to the Lord and was born again. Enthusiasm for the things of God led her to spend much of her time at church, and she found great healing there until one of the staff members began an inappropriate and controlling relationship with her.

She moved away to college and spiraled into depression. However, rather than giving up, she looked up. She garnered the courage to seek help. She stayed in church and went to counseling. It was not an easy process, but she stuck with it and has now come out on the other side as a productive Christian. She does not blame God or other people for her pain. She has refused to remain a victim. In fact, she is a teacher now. She finds she has tremendous love for her students because of what she has been through. God gives her opportunities to love the unlovable and protect them from hurt. The same comfort she received from the Lord she is now able to pass on to others.

Where many would remain hard and bitter, she is sincerely grateful for how God has redeemed her past. Sometimes there is still pain, but now that pain is bearing fruit in the lives of others. She is seeing God's purpose in her problems. She is letting her wounds become windows. So can you.

Often the main focus of our life ministries will come out of our specific areas of hurt. Sometimes they won't. That is for God to decide. But whatever ministry you are in, you will find that the hurts that once occupied a large part of your soul have now become reservoirs of wisdom and mercy for others.

We can grow through our valleys and minister to others. We can discover that the areas where we were hit the hardest have become our strengths—perhaps even our greatest assets. We can find ourselves able to speak directly into someone else's situation, knowing exactly what they are thinking and feeling, and recognizing the path God will use to lead them out. We too can be part of seeing God use something for good that the enemy meant for harm.

Chapter 10

Take Off Your Bib,
Put On Your Apron

Lying in the hospital bed is a woman who has been in pain for two years straight, almost without reprieve. Doctors have gradually increased the strength and frequency of painkillers, but nothing seems to work. Day in and day out she lies there, so distracted by pain that even watching television or reading a book is impossible. Explosions of pain run up and down her back and across her limbs. Friends and relatives visit her and sit by her side, sharing comfort and reassurance, and she experiences a little relief for a while. But when they leave, she is alone with her aching body. She goes to sleep dreading the moment she will wake up.

Then one day she wakes up, and the pain has lessened. One of the many experimental drugs the doctors have been trying has actually worked, and the effect is miraculous. She feels like sitting up. She eats a normal meal, then looks out the window and notices the beauty of the trees and flowers for what seems like the first time. The next day, the pain has ebbed even further away, and by the next week it is only a memory. She is free. Soon, she walks out of the hospital, family by her side, ready to live again.

Take Off Your Bib, Put On Your Apron

Doesn't it feel like a new lease on life when pain we thought would never end is suddenly gone? Leaving the valley brings great relief, and getting the right perspective on our scars and our pain offers a big advantage—but there is more to life than getting well. Getting out of the hospital may seem like the end of a long nightmare, but it is actually the beginning of a new life. There is a season of service ahead of us, and often that season begins where our pain left off.

This is no small matter, for some people see their highest calling in life as being free from life's pains and struggles.

- "I want a good marriage."
- "I want my body healed."
- "I want prosperity."
- "I want to be happy."
- "I want to be holy."
- "I want my life to honor God."

Is there anything wrong with those things? No, except for the "I" part. The church is more than the "healthy, wealthy, happy, holy club." Some of us need to wake up and realize that God wants to heal, restore and get us back on track—but not just to make us feel better. He has a purpose for us.

There are two stages of healing. If you suffer a serious injury, the first step is going to the hospital where you are put in bed and told, "Stay in bed! Don't move." The doctors and nurses treat you, mending what has been broken, and then they expect you to stay still and rest.

Soon, however, sometimes right after surgery, they want you to start moving around a little bit. Step two has begun. And not long after that—in fact, as soon as possible—the doctors expect you to get out of bed and start walking again. This is a vital part of the healing process. If you lay there in bed, scared or simply unwilling to get up, your condition will only get worse.

There is a season after being hurt to lie down and allow the healing to begin. But that is only step one. Step two involves activity. Without activity, muscles begin to atrophy. Too many believers are so focused on getting healed they never see the purpose behind the healing. God did not bring the Israelites out of Egypt just to deliver them from their pain and bondage, but rather to lead them into the Promised Land. Manna in the wilderness is not God's best; it is a temporary stopgap until dwelling in a land flowing with milk and honey.

If people waited until they felt like getting out of the hospital bed before they actually got up, hardly anybody would ever leave the hospital. A few aches and pains may remain, and muscles may be weak and sore from inactivity. What is needed is not a longer hospital stay, but activity. For the Christian, it is taking some steps of faith. The completion of our healing is not found in passively waiting for God to "finish the job" so we can get up, but rather in strengthening ourselves in the Lord by pursuing His purpose.

Many believers use their season of healing as an excuse to stay in the hospital bed, so to speak.

- "I'd like to help with the children's ministry, but I was hurt. My pastor took off with his secretary. I poured my life into that church. I don't know if I can trust any leader again. I'm not ready to jump back into the work of the Lord just yet."

- "Maybe some day I'll get plugged into that Sunday school class, but right now the wounds of my divorce are still too fresh. Give me a few more years."

- "I know I have a calling to work with youth, but sometimes I still get attacked with depression. I think I'll wait until I have that conquered."

The sad irony is that while we are waiting on God, He is waiting on us.

There is a precious lady in our church who has been confined to a wheelchair for most of her adult life. Getting out of the house has become increasingly difficult for her. Even making it to church on Sunday is an adventure. Sometimes she can't make it.

If anyone would seem to have a right to sit alone at home feeling sorry for herself, she would. She has the perfect excuse for staying in bed. But she doesn't stay there. She calls people on the phone who desperately need attention, and more recently she has used the Internet to minister to others. When people say to her, "Well, you're probably too busy to listen to my problems," she lovingly replies, "No, I've got the time."

If you stay in your spiritual hospital bed for too long, you will die. If you wait until you are 100 percent better, you will never get up.

You say, "But it hurts to move."

It's hurting you worse to stay put.

"But I have all these scars."

In God's plan, those are trophies.

CHOSEN FOR A PURPOSE

God has called us out to bring us in. He has healed us for a purpose. He has transformed us to use us for His glory. You have probably heard of David's mighty men—elite warriors who helped him guide Israel during his reign. Did you know what these mighty men looked like when they first came to David?

> All those who were in distress or in debt or discontented gathered around him, and he became their leader.
>
> —1 SAMUEL 22:2

What a motley crew! Who could build a winning team out of people with no confidence, no self-respect, no money and no influence? These men were losers with a capital L.

I am sure they had their reasons—life had not been fair; their family had betrayed them; they were victims of false accusations—whatever.

God used David to put these men back together again, and by the time David was finished with them, they had become giant-slayers. It is miraculous enough that they got out of debt, began to feel better about themselves and recovered broken relationships. The real miracle, however, is found not simply in their personal restoration, but in their lives of heroic service to the king.

For example, did you know that Goliath had a brother? That's right, his name was Lahmi, and he was just as big and just as bad as Goliath. Who killed him? Not David, but one of David's mighty men, one who had at one time been a big-time loser. (See 1 Chronicles 20:5.) This is just one among the many exploits of David's mighty men. David didn't have to kill all the giants himself anymore. He had multiplied himself in the lives of others.

In the same way that David chose those men, God has chosen you to be part of His army. He wants you to be a giant-slayer. Your past may be no better than that of the men who first gathered around David in the cave. You may only see pain; God sees potential. You may see yourself as a wimp; God sees you as a warrior. You may see a victim; God sees a victor. Others think you're a chump; God thinks you're a champ.

Paul told the Corinthians:

> Brothers, think of what you were when you were called. Not many of you were wise by human standards; not many were influential; not many were of noble birth. But God chose the foolish things of the world to shame

the wise; God chose the weak things of the world to shame the strong.

—1 CORINTHIANS 1:26–27

I think God gets a kick out creating a winning team from what looks like, for all intents and purposes, a group of losers. He can take a group of unskilled, unmotivated and unimpressive people and turn them into an elite fighting force—scarier to the enemy than Navy Seals and the Green Berets. You and I have been called out of our situation, sometimes a very painful one, to do great exploits for our King.

The Greek word for church, *ekklesia,* literally means "called-out ones." So when Jesus said, "I will build My church," He wasn't talking about steeples and stained-glass windows. He was talking about us—His called-out ones. "I will build my called-out ones, and the gates of hell shall not prevail against them."

Why has He chosen us? Not simply to get us out of debt or free from stress or delivered from our circumstances. He has handpicked us to multiply His work—preach the good news, heal the sick, cast out devils, do mighty exploits and build His kingdom.

Israel was called out of Egypt, not to wander in the wilderness, but to dwell in the Promised Land and be a light to the nations. We too have been called out of slavery to the principles of this world to be a light to our neighbors, friends, relatives and coworkers.

ACTIVE DUTY

Following are testimonies of individuals in our church who are now actively serving the Lord, allowing Him to use their hurts to bring healing to others. They have taken off the bib and put on the apron.

Anita

Anita, a woman in our church, was engaged to be married, but tragically her fiancé died. Though it was difficult, she eventually recovered from the blow. God rewarded her perseverance and brought another marvelous man into her life. They married, and now they serve in our church as altar workers.

One Sunday morning, one of our greeters noticed a mother and daughter come in, and the daughter appeared distraught. The mother requested prayer for the daughter and explained that the man she was going to marry had just died. The young woman was understandably devastated.

The greeter led the women to Anita, not knowing about Anita's past. When Anita learned of the young woman's situation, she was able to minister to her with firsthand knowledge of the pain she was going through. Like Esther, Anita became God's handmaiden "for such a time as this."

What if Anita had still been nursing her wounds and had neglected to join the altar ministry? Her hurt would have been wasted at that moment.

Wounded pastor

There is another man, a former pastor, who was wounded by his own sin and was forced to leave the ministry.

"I walked into your church a broken person," he wrote in his testimony. "I had no hope for tomorrow and was justifying my sins. I had been a pastor for thirteen years and had fallen into moral failure. I felt abandoned by God. I had lost my income and my friends, and I was desperately looking for a church. At one place I visited, an elder told me I was too high profile to attend there. I felt the body of Christ had disconnected from me. I felt like an embarrassment to the body."

This pastor came to our church, and thankfully God had something for him there. He began to heal and regain his trust.

He wrote me, "I am now blessed to have a wife who loves me, supports me and encourages me. I have children who love me, a job that pays me well and a brand-new home. God does restore the broken. I can confess that I am a man of destiny. God's fingerprint is on my heart, and He is preparing me for ministry again. I see a future where I can function as a healthy part of the body of Christ. My wounds still exist, but they serve only as a reminder of where I came from."

I know he is on the road to full recovery because he is not focused on his own needs; he sees himself becoming a servant once more.

Ben

One of the people who help run our twelve-step program for recovering addicts is himself a trophy of God's grace. Ben was born into a family where his earliest memories are of his parent's constant drinking and fighting. When he was a young child they divorced, and Ben went to live with one of his father's relatives, a Christian widow. As a teenager, he gave his heart to the Lord at a Billy Graham crusade, but he didn't really understand the commitment he had made. When he later went to live with his grandparents, bad habits got hold of his life, and he made friends who were only concerned with partying.

Ben discovered alcohol at a school dance, and he felt his fears dissipate the more he drank. Not long thereafter his mother died of cancer and his father of a heart attack, leaving Ben alone. Drinking seemed to numb the pain of yesterday and to give him confidence for today. Who cared about tomorrow? The bottle would end up being his companion for the next twenty years.

He also began to use drugs to fill the void, and eventually he attempted suicide. Finally, Ben cried out to Jesus and was spared. With the help of a treatment program, Ben fought back one step at a time. He married his girlfriend and joined our church, where he now leads a weekly recovery meeting.

Ben has a lot of things he could be angry with God about. Why was he born into such a dysfunctional family? Why did his parents have to suffer untimely deaths? Where was God during his own twenty-year sojourn into drug hell? Even if he chose not to be bitter, Ben could have chosen to stay a baby Christian, constantly focused on having his needs met. But he didn't stay in the spiritual high chair. After he found the answer, he let God bring him to a place of maturity and service where he is now impacting hundreds of lives. His own testimony has become a lighthouse from which Jesus shines forth.

PUT ON YOUR APRON

God wants to turn our problem into provision, our mess into a message and our test into a testimony. How can He do that if we stay in the hospital bed? What good are we there?

When we are baby Christians, or when we are recovering from hurts, there are times that God waits on us hand and foot. We are treated like infants, and every time we cry, God seems to come immediately to our rescue. We need someone to change our diapers, powder our bottoms and give us a bottle. We ring the bell, and God comes running. We wear our bib and come to church with mouths open wide, like a baby bird in the nest.

Then one day we ring the bell, and God doesn't come running. We wonder what is wrong. Does God hear us? Does He still love us? Does He still care?

Ready or not, God is moving us to the next stage in our development. He is in effect saying, "It's time to grow up. I am going to teach you that you don't ring the bell and I come running. *I* ring the bell, and *you* come running because I am the Lord. I'm not your servant; you are *My* servant. It is time to grow up. There are giants to be killed, exploits to be done and blessings to be gained."

Maybe you are at that point right now. You may feel that God is not answering your prayers—at least not as He used to. You're beginning to wonder what is wrong. Perhaps nothing is wrong. It is just growing pains—you are learning who rings the bell. You need to take off our bib and put on your apron. It is time to serve the Lord. We are no longer baby birds, but mighty eagles.

Chapter 11

How to Turn
a Little Into a Lot

"I have nothing to offer God." I hear that a lot. And sometimes it's true. Our past, though not without its share of
struggles, may seem unspectacular. Our testimonies are not
gory enough to be interesting, much less useful to anybody.
Our current situation can be summed up as follows: no
money, no spouse, no job, no faith, no future and no
prospects of any kind. In short, you may think, *I'm a nobody
with nothing going nowhere. How can God use that?*

God specializes in turning nothing into something. He
doesn't even need any ingredients to work with. When
human beings create things, we create things with existing
material. We make a cake by mixing ingredients together—
flour, eggs, milk and so forth. We make computers out of
plastic and metals.

God creates things out of nothing, or as the theologians
who love to use their Latin put it, *ex nihilo.* The Hebrew word
bara is used in Genesis 1, "In the beginning God created..."
The word *bara* means "to create something out of nothing."
God spoke, "Let there be light," and boom—light suddenly
existed. No concoction of existing materials necessary—just

the force of His word. If current science is correct, the creative commands of God are still being obeyed today as the universe continues to expand at an amazing rate.

If God can do that, your situation is neither too boring nor too hopeless. Most of us remember the first Indiana Jones movie, *Raiders of the Lost Ark*. At the end of the movie, the Nazis open the ark and find nothing inside but sand. Oh yeah, and a few flying destructive angels—or demons—or whatever those things were. Well, that's Hollywood.

But do you remember what was inside the real ark of the covenant? Three important items:

- The Ten Commandments—the original top ten list
- Leftover manna from Israel's wilderness adventure
- Aaron's rod that blossomed

These three items symbolized the Word of God, the provision of God and the power of God. It is easily seen how the Ten Commandments reveal His will and the manna His supernatural sustenance, but what does a rod have to do with His ability?

While the Israelites were traveling in the wilderness, God had the leaders of the twelve tribes place their rods in the tabernacle, with Aaron's rod representing the tribe of Levi. The next day when Moses entered the tabernacle, Aaron's rod, that dead piece of wood, had budded, just as if still attached to a living tree. (See Numbers 17:1–9.) Where there was no possibility of life, God brought life. God was bringing life out of death—a foretaste of the resurrection of Christ. That rod was God's promise to Israel and all humanity that He can make something out of our lives no matter what our situation is. If God made Aaron's rod bud, He can make a "blooming something" out of your life!

In 2 Kings 4 we find a poor woman who had nothing. Her

husband, who had been from the school of the prophets (basically, a Bible college student), was dead. The widow had two boys to feed but was so behind financially that she was going to lose them to slavery in order to pay off her debt. She had nothing, and the little she did have was in danger of being lost. Back in those days it was precarious for a woman to lose her husband because, unless she had enough money stored up to make it, she could easily end up a beggar or, worse yet, a prostitute.

She was scared and begged Elisha for help. He said to her, "How can I help you? Tell me, what do you have in your house?" (v. 2).

She answered, "Your servant has nothing there at all, except a little oil."

Her first thought was that she had absolutely nothing, but that was not quite true; she did have a little something. But then again, what good is a little oil? It's as good as nothing— or so she thought. I wouldn't presume to call this woman a whiner; she really did face a threatening problem. Still, her response shows that she was more focused on the problem than on any solution God might have. She didn't realize that a little is much in the hands of a miracle-working God.

I will never forget a gathering I attended that was sponsored by the singles' ministry at our church. I was talking to people, and I noticed one girl sitting on the couch all by herself. People were trying to strike up conversation with her, but apparently without success. I am shy by nature and know what it is like to feel uncomfortable in a social setting, so I thought maybe that was her problem, too. I took her on as sort of a project— maybe I could help her feel more comfortable.

As we began to talk, I immediately realized that she was one of the worst whiners I had ever met. It did not take long for her to start rehearsing what was wrong with her life.

Whenever I would say something upbeat, she would reply in long, drawn-out whiny syllables, "Well, that's the problem." She reminded me of the whiner family skits they used to do on *Saturday Night Live.*

I said, "Tell me about your problem, and I will see if I can help you."

She answered me and listed her many problems, "I am ugly, and no one likes me. I don't have a boyfriend. In fact, I don't have any friends."

I replied, "I couldn't help but notice that you were just sitting on the couch. I saw people trying to come up and talk to you, and you didn't seem to respond. People might like to be your friend if you would just talk to them."

I could have predicted her reply: "Well, that's the problem."

She went through this problem and that problem, and I kept giving her specific suggestions.

"That's the problem. I don't have a car."

"That's the problem. I don't have any extra money."

"That's the problem. I don't have a license."

No matter what I said, her response was the same. She had a problem for every solution.

Although they would never admit it, and maybe they are not even consciously aware of it, some people grow accustomed to their problems to the point that they do not really want a solution. As funny as it might sound, their identity comes from the problems they complain about. Their problems actually become a security blanket—life may not be fun or enjoyable, but at least it is safe and predictable. The whiner uses whining to control. As long as you allow people to control with their whining, they will not stop.

We don't know if this widow was a whiner, but there was an edge of complaint on her reply. Complaining and whining about not having anything lead to inactivity. For

her own good, then, God involves her in the solution.
Elisha directs her:

> Go around and ask all your neighbors for empty jars.
> Don't ask for just a few. Then go inside and shut the
> door behind you and your sons. Pour oil into all the jars,
> and as each is filled, put it to one side.
>
> —2 KINGS 4:3–4

What an odd plan. The widow has almost nothing, and
what is she supposed to do? Go out and collect more of—
well, nothing. Empty vessels. The widow was about to find
out what God can do with nothing. She did what the prophet
said, and miraculously the oil kept flowing until every jar
was filled to the brim. She probably wished now she had collected more of nothing. She sold the oil to pay her debts,
and she and her sons lived on the rest.

TURNING A LITTLE INTO A LOT

God can turn a little into a lot and create something out of
nothing. There are six things this story teaches us that we
need to learn and do.

1. God is ready to help, but He is going to use you.

The widow initially wanted Elisha to take care of everything for her. She was hoping to hear him say, "Honey, your
husband was such a good man that I'm really going to make
this my project. Go to bed, and when you wake up in the
morning, I will have taken care of everything."

We expect the same kind of help from God. If we are having
financial struggles, we say, "C'mon, God, I've been tithing. I've
been going to church. I've been a good person. Take care of
my finances." We want to wake up the next morning, go to
our mailbox and discover a check for $100,000.

Ephesians 3:20 does say God is "able to do exceedingly abundantly above all that we ask or think." But the next part says, "According to the power that works in us" (NKJV). The clear implication is that God is going to use you and what you have, however little, to bring about your breakthrough.

Elisha didn't just say, "Here's the money. Go home and relax." God's plan involved the widow; without her stepping out in faith and doing the work, the miracle would not have occurred.

As a father, I have discovered this same principle. I am a house expert on things like art, literature and writing term papers. The kids come to me and say, "Dad, I need help on this paper. What do you think?" What they are really saying is, "Dad, would you think of an idea for a paper and give me a plot and then give me the characters and then maybe write a few words?" They think they have nothing—no ideas and no writing skills.

I know they have more than they think they have. Therefore, to their initial disappointment, I refuse to do everything for them. I could, and the paper would probably be better than one they could write themselves, but it wouldn't be theirs. If they are going to grow and mature, they need to learn how to do it themselves. I make the kids do as much as they can do before I will help. Sometimes they say, "Forget it then, Dad." However, if they decide to do it my way, they always come back later and thank me.

God's kids are no different. We want Him to do our homework for us. We want God to do all the work and we get the A. But like any good father, God insists, "I'm going to involve you. Give it your best effort, and I will help you." He may even force us to look harder and discover that we do, after all, have a little something. It may seem to us to be of no value or significance, but God is about to turn our little into a lot.

2. Everybody has something.

Elisha said to the widow, "Tell me, what do you have in your house?" Tommy Barnett wrote a well-known book that proclaimed there is a miracle in your house. The only problem is that sometimes we can't see it. The widow knew she had a little bit of oil, but she had no idea that oil would become the source of her miracle.

I want to tell you that there is a miracle in your marriage. There is a miracle in your body. There is a miracle in your business. There is a miracle in your house. If nothing else, you still have breath. And where there is breath, there is hope. One of my favorite verses in the Bible confirms this.

> Anyone who is among the living has hope—even a live dog is better off than a dead lion!
>
> —ECCLESIASTES 9:4

3. Use what you have.

I read about an inmate who escaped from prison by braiding dental floss into the rope he used to scale the fence. I don't rejoice that a criminal escaped, but I do admire his creative tenacity.[1]

God loves to create, and if you offer Him something—anything—you will be surprised at what He can make of it. If you want more, be faithful with what you have. You have a measure of faith—use it. You are breathing. You are alive. God can work with that.

Sitting around doing nothing is the worst thing to do. Some Christians excuse their inactivity by claiming, "I am waiting on the Lord to renew my strength." The word *wait* in the Hebrew means "to serve." Our English word has the same connotation. When you go to a restaurant, the people that serve you are called waiters and waitresses. They don't sit back in the kitchen and watch the world go by, just hanging out until you somehow get their attention. They are supposed to serve you. Even before you order, a good waiter is busy preparing your table, pouring water and making sure everything is satisfactory.

That is exactly how you should wait upon the Lord. Before you ever receive His order, you should be examining yourself according to the Word to make sure everything is satisfactory. You might say, "I haven't found the right opportunity yet. I don't have all the resources." Then serve God with what you have.

4. Exercise your faith.

The widow did two things that precipitated her miracle. First, in the midst of her doubt and fears, she listened to the prophet—she heard the word of the Lord. In that hearing, faith began to rise. Romans 10:17 says, "Faith cometh by hearing, and hearing by the word of God" (KJV).

Second, she acted on that word, collecting the empty jars as Elisha had ordered. Put simply, she heard and she did. As the old hymn puts it, "Trust and obey." Before long, her faith grew, doubt and fear diminished, and the miracle blossomed.

Whenever we think we have too little, or nothing at all, doubt and fear attack our faith. Though not exclusively, doubt tends to be the biggest struggle for those who are more intellectually bent. By that I do not mean they are smarter; they just filter the data of life first through their brains. They analyze, scrutinize and size up the situation. "The facts just don't add up. I am never going to make it!" They suffer from the proverbial "paralysis of analysis."

Others, just as smart, do not analyze as much as they feel. They handle the situation intuitively sensing that things are hopeless. Fear grips them.

Whether you lean more toward analysis or intuition, and all of us have some mixture of both, the antidote is the same—faith. If the situation is too much for you, with doubt and fear towering overhead, hear the Word and do the Word. That is where faith comes from and how faith grows.

I have been working out at the gym now for about ten years. Before that, although I had always been an athlete, I was pathetically out of shape. The only part of me that was decent was my right forearm because I played a lot of tennis. In fact, I looked like Popeye. My forearm was literally bigger than my biceps and triceps. But other than that, I was a wimp. I had become the ninety-eight-pound weakling—OK, so it was more than ninety-eight pounds.

I didn't realize how out of shape and weak I had become until one day when I picked up a twenty-pound weight and could not curl it even once with my left arm. Soon after that my son, who was thirteen at the time, challenged me to arm wrestle and handily beat me. Feeling humiliated, I decided to think about working out. I wasn't yet ready to actually exercise, mind you, but I was thinking about it.

I remember sitting at home watching exercise shows. The workout leaders were always encouraging: "You're doing great! Keep it up!" And there I was sitting on the couch.

That's what some Christians do. They go to church and watch other people exercise their faith, ministry or gift. Like a fitness instructor, the pastor is up front shouting encouraging words, "You are able to do all things through Christ who strengthens you."

Two years earlier, my wife had given me a lifetime membership to a local health club, but I had not gone even once. The longer I had waited, the less I had wanted to go because I was embarrassed at how out of shape I was. When I finally did slink in the doors, my greatest fears were confirmed. Everyone else knew where to go and what to do, and I couldn't even find the restrooms. In my eyes all the men looked like professional bodybuilders and the women aerobic champions. Talk about grasshopper mentality—I was intimidated.

I was tempted to go home and watch television. But as I began to work out, I gained more confidence, and soon I felt neither inadequate nor intimidated. It wasn't easy, but it was worth it.

"Faith cometh by hearing, and hearing by the word of God" (Rom. 10:17, KJV). If you want to increase your faith, use what faith you have. If you want to increase your muscles, use them. Don't just pray that God will give you bigger muscles—He won't. And don't wait to work out until you get strong enough—that's backward, and you will only get weaker. In the same way, don't wait for great faith to rise up in you before you try to increase it. Use what you have!

Years later, I am certainly no bodybuilder, but I am much stronger than I used to be. I can now curl thirty-pound weights at least thirty times. On the bench, I can easily do three sets of ten with one hundred fifty pounds. For a lot of men, that's not that much, but compared to what I used to do, I am Arnold Schwarzenegger. Like the widow, I took the little I had and watched it increase.

It was the same way years ago when I would practice preaching in the mirror. I knew God had called me into the ministry, but I hated speaking in front of people. There was nothing in life I feared more than public speaking. I cannot tell you how many times I blushed, stuttered and shook my way through oral book reports at school. It was so embarrassing to me that I would try to get sick and miss school that day. I would sunburn myself at the beach on purpose so people would not know I was blushing while I was giving my presentation.

So when God called me to preach, I had a long way to go. But practicing in the mirror helped. At first I would get embarrassed, and no one was even there! But I built my faith and my skills, and soon found that I could preach in front of a crowd. I started with nothing, gave what little I did have to God and my faith increased.

Once I surrendered to His call, I thought God would solve my problem in one glorious instant, but He didn't. I went through college intentionally taking speech classes, although I didn't have to for my major. I took them to get over the fear of public speaking. It was a humiliating process, and for the first year or two, I blushed and stammered and shook like a grade-school kid, but I just kept doing it. I distinctly remember thinking, *God, I sure hope I have heard from You. I am making the biggest fool of myself for nothing if I haven't.*

God often uses us at the point where we are the weakest, perhaps so we have to rely on Him and His strength can shine through us. I was blessed when I finally heard about Winston Churchill, one of the greatest orators in history. Some historians credit his speaking skills for keeping Great Britain going during the darkest days of the Nazi bombings in World War II. Years later, a reporter asked him, "Mr. Churchill, you never get nervous when you speak, do you?" His reply both surprised and encouraged me, "I get nervous every time before I speak. But I have learned to channel my nervousness into energy."

I still get nervous every week before speaking to my own church. Sometimes I ask my wife if she has heard from God and wants to preach, but usually it falls to me. I have learned to channel my nervousness into energy. Thank God He has taken me further than I ever expected, but it would not have happened if I had not used the little He gave me.

5. *Do not be afraid to ask, and ask big.*

Elisha told the widow, "Ask all your neighbors for empty jars. Don't ask for just a few." James 4:2 says, "You do not have, because you do not ask God."

Americans typically do not like to ask for help. Males especially like to view themselves as "self-made men." To ask for help from anyone, be it God or man, is humbling. It points us to our need and dependence. It is embarrassing to admit that we don't have enough. For sure, some would rather die than expose their own need.

I don't think this passage is encouraging us to bum what we need off other people, but I do believe the prophet's plan provided the widow with a way to break out of the confinement of her own inadequacies into the abundance of God. We too need to break out of our limitations by asking for God's help.

A single mother in our congregation was struggling to raise her girls on the welfare check she received from the government. She told me, "After paying rent and light and gas, I barely had enough to buy our necessities. Frustration, anger and hatred had built up in my heart. I had become a woman who hated life itself."

She came to church, rededicated her life to the Lord and heard God speak to her about getting off welfare. She said, "I let my pride down and asked for help from my parents so I could get out from where I was and do something with my life. I graduated from college and got hired before I even finished my intern hours. It is a good paying job. Letting go of all the anger, hatred and bitterness has brought so many blessings our way."

John Wesley said God does nothing except in response to prayer. I believe that. We can and should do other things than pray, but we should do nothing without prayer. Our solution will come by asking God, and sometimes others, for help. And as long as we're asking, let's ask big! God is both able and willing. Remember, the oil didn't stop flowing until the widow ran out of jars.

6. *Do what He says.*

If the widow had balked and not collected the jars, she would have stopped God's miracle in its tracks. The plan seemed, on the surface, absurd. She had nearly nothing and is supposed to collect jars full of nothing. More often than not, the first steps toward our solution seem illogical. We simply cannot figure out how in the world doing what God said to do is going to help. That's where faith comes in—and action.

When God tells you what to do—do it. You may be asking God for some insight that will get your business off the ground, and you are hearing Him say, "Take your wife out to dinner and start treating her right." You reply, "I am not talking about my marriage. I am talking about my business."

It may not make any sense to us, but God's answer might be the key to unlock success in business.

Sometimes God want us to praise Him in the midst of battle. I must admit that this is hard for me. When I am stressed, trying to figure out solutions to impossible problems, the last thing I want to hear is," Well, just praise the Lord." Though I know it is wrong, I like to complain and groan as I work hard serving Him. Just when my old nature is getting the upper hand, my wife walks in and says, "Jim, let's pray about it. Let's praise the Lord. Don't you listen to your own preaching?" About this time I want to pull a Jackie Gleason: "To the moon, Alice." That's because deep down in my heart I know she is right and that God's plan of action is not always what I want to do.

In fact, the very first thing God tells us to do is probably the thing we won't want to do. But if we balk, we will stop the miracle in its tracks. It may not make sense, but we must do what He says to get the outcome He wants.

How to Turn a Little Into a Lot

GOD IS WILLING TO GO AS FAR WITH YOU
AS YOU ARE WILLING TO GO WITH HIM

When did the oil stop? When the jars were full. I imagine that later on the widow wished she had collected more jars. God went as far with her as she was willing to go with Him. He met her measure of faith.

Do you ever wonder why some people always seem to be more blessed than you? Does God like them more? Are they just lucky? Maybe they know something you don't know—some secret insight into the mysteries of God. Actually, they just went the extra mile and discovered that God hadn't lost His breath—He was right there with them.

How many jars of faith have you collected? Two? Two will be filled. Ten? Then ten will be filled. A thousand? Then a thousand will be filled.

GOD USES NOBODIES

God can make something out of nothing. He can turn a little into a lot. And He specializes in using nobodies. God can do great feats and miracles in the lives of people who know they are nobody better than he can through people who think they are somebody.

I think of Moses, the little Hebrew baby born in Egypt when all boy babies were being killed. Moses was a class-A nobody, born to a slave, until God raised him up, even as an infant, and had him raised in the household of Pharaoh.

D. L. Moody said that for the first forty years of Moses' life he thought he was somebody. By the time he hit his forties, he was no longer strutting around Pharaoh's house; he was shuffling through fields watching over his father-in-law's sheep. He didn't even have his own flock. So for the next forty years he learned that he was a nobody. But God wasn't through with him, and during the last forty years of his life Moses discovered how much God could use a nobody.

This final transition began with a rather dramatic call of God.

> Now Moses was tending the flock of Jethro his father-in-law, the priest of Midian, and he led the flock to the far side of the desert and came to Horeb, the mountain of God. There the angel of the LORD appeared to him in flames of fire from within a bush. Moses saw that though the bush was on fire it did not burn up. So Moses thought, "I will go over and see this strange sight—why the bush does not burn up."
>
> When the LORD saw that he had gone over to look, God called to him from within the bush, "Moses! Moses!"
>
> And Moses said, "Here I am."
>
> "Do not come any closer," God said, "Take off your sandals, for the place where you are standing is holy ground." Then he said, "I am the God of your father, the God of Abraham, the God of Isaac, and the God of Jacob." At this, Moses hid his face, because he was afraid to look at God.
>
> —EXODUS 3:1–7

There are three things about the call of Moses that apply to you and me.

God uses the ordinary to produce the extraordinary.

Leonard Ravenhill told the story about a group of American tourists who were traveling through Europe. While they were touring one particularly quaint and picturesque village, they saw an old man sitting beside a fence. One of the American tourists asked the old man, "Were any great men born in this village?" The old man rubbed his beard and thought for a moment and said, "No. Only babies."

We all start out ordinary until God decides to touch us, set us apart and give us a purpose in life. Great Christians are not born. Even Billy Graham and other giants of the faith started their spiritual walk in diapers. There are no blue-bloods in the kingdom of God. We are all ordinary vessels that God uses to produce extraordinary results.

God reveals Himself to seekers.

While it may have initially only been curiosity, Moses took the time and effort to check things out. God rewards pursuit. Jesus said it like this:

> Ask and it will be given to you; seek and you will find; knock and the door will be opened to you.
>
> —MATTHEW 7:7

The words *ask, seek* and *knock* in the original language all have the meaning of continuous action. In other words, "Ask and keep on asking; seek and keep on seeking; knock and keep on knocking." If you do, the answers will come, the lost will be found, and the door will be opened. God rewards the diligent seeker, not the casual observer.

Moses might have seen the bush and kept on trucking. That is what most people do. I would guess that at least half of the people in any given church on Sunday morning are not seekers but casual observers. If we are typical Americans, we will go to church as long as it is easy, convenient and fits into our schedule. The moment the going gets tough, forget it.

Where do the great men and women of God come from? The answer is quite simple: They come from the same place we are right now. But when God calls, they pursue Him with all of their hearts. They are ordinary people who are willing to pay the price and pray the price. They are willing to go as far with God as He is willing to go with them. They don't let God moments—those windows of opportunity—pass them by.

When God begins to move, stop and look. Go investigate. Be intrigued by the nearness and glory of God as He moves among His people. People have missed past moves of God because they were not drawn to the flame. I am sure that there were people living during the time of Christ who saw Him walk down their streets, but they were too busy getting dinner ready for their family, puttering around the garage or relaxing on the deck to follow Him.

Moses probably had a hundred things that seemed more pressing, but not one of them was as important as finding out why that bush was burning and not being consumed. God promises to reward seekers and those who go after what He is doing.

God's presence makes us worthy.

God told Moses to take off his shoes because he was standing on holy ground. When God calls us, He qualifies us. I don't know about you, but I have never felt good enough, knowledgeable enough, skilled enough or prepared enough for what God has called me to do. Never. Not once. He must see something in me I don't see in myself.

We do not make ourselves holy enough for God and then do things for Him. God makes us holy by His presence. Not one of us is worthy on our own. When we lift holy hands, it is because He has made them holy. Each one of us is a candidate for service because God makes us holy.

Are you a nobody? Welcome to the club. Do you have nothing to offer? Many of us feel the same way. It is time to put those concerns aside and let God turn nothing into something, and a little into a lot.

Chapter 12

How God Handles Excuses

What would you do for God if you could do anything? What would you be for God if you could be anything? What is holding you back? Why do we sometimes fall short of God's best for our lives?

Almost all Christians say they want God to heal their hurts and use them for His glory. Still, when He comes calling we commonly heap up excuses. We quickly discover that it is easier to talk about what we want to do than to do it.

Moses made a lot of excuses when God called him to a new line of work—leading God's chosen flock, the Israelites, out of Egypt. Moses had been working as a shepherd, but leading sheep and leading people are two totally different things. Did God really think he had the resumé to accomplish such a daunting task? Why him? Why now? Why this?

It is amazing how much we question God. First, we wonder why we have to go through the valleys. Then we wonder why He doesn't deliver us and use us in ministry. Finally, when He does call us into ministry, we wonder, *Why me? Surely He has the wrong person.*

God had an answer for every one of Moses' excuses. Since we have not come up with any better excuses in the last several thousand years, His responses still speak to us today.

"WHO AM I?"

Moses' first response to God's call was, "You have to be kidding me."

> Who am I, that I should go to Pharaoh and bring the Israelites out of Egypt?
>
> —EXODUS 3:11

Most of us somehow think we know more about ourselves than God does. If He only knew the real us—our hurts, fears and insecurities—He would know better. The fact is, we are nobody until God calls us, but when He does, we can rest assured that He will give us everything we need to succeed.

I remember my response when God called me into the ministry. "Me? No way! There must be millions—no, billions—of people out there who could do a better job than me." I was being neither humble nor obstinate—just truthful.

Moses wasn't sure he had what it took to do what God was calling him to do. He was afraid he might fail, afraid he might let his people down, afraid he didn't have the clout that this particular task required. What is the antidote to fear? The presence of God. God simply said, "I will be with you."

When I was a little boy, my parents would drop my two brothers and me off at our grandparents' house so that they could have a date night. We loved going to Grandma and Grandpa's. The time would pass quickly as we would eat, play and watch television. And though we dreaded it, eventually the time would come for us to go to bed. "But we want to go to sleep at home, in our own beds and with Mom and Dad," we would complain. Grandma and Grandpa would explain, "There is nothing to be afraid of. Your parents will be back to pick you up and take you home to your own beds. You need to get to sleep."

With the promise of Mom and Dad's return, we would eventually fall asleep. One of my precious childhood memories is the feeling of being slightly awakened in my dad's powerful arms with a blanket wrapped around me. Being the oldest and the biggest child, my feet would typically stick out from the blanket. I can still feel the cold, damp, foggy air hitting my feet. More importantly, I can still feel the warmth of my dad's loving arms taking me home. When Dad was there, everything was OK.

As I grew up in church, it was easy for me to think of God as my loving heavenly Father—someone who would carry me without fail, wrap me in warmth and bring me to a safe place. It was many years later that I realized many people don't have such a view of their father. Precious sisters in the Lord have told me, "Pastor, if my father put his hands around me while I was sleeping, it was not to bless me but to abuse me."

In the closing scene of the movie *Carrie,* the lead character is taking flowers to the grave when suddenly hands shoot up from the dirt to grab her. She wakes up screaming—it was a nightmare. That closing sequence was a scary and startling scene, but it was only a movie. Sadly, in real life, because of abuse, neglect or a host of other family dysfunctions, some people are still feeling the grip of their father's failures although he has been dead for years.

Without minimizing anyone's experience with his or her earthly father, I can say with confidence that God is entirely good. He is a loving Father who with one touch can dispel all fear. No wonder time and again in the Bible our heavenly Father says, "Fear not, for I am with you."

"I WON'T KNOW WHAT TO SAY"

Moses then throws out this excuse: "How will I know what to say? What if they ask me questions I can't answer, like what Your name is? By the way, what is Your name?" I picture him starting to bargain a bit: "Suppose I do go—then what?"

I remember one time when I felt the Lord speak to me at a movie theater. He said, "Go witness to the girl behind the candy counter."

I was not in the mood for ministry, so I said, "Who, me?"

God said, "Yes, you. I will be with you."

I still didn't want to do it, so I complained, "C'mon, God, give me a break. I'm on my date night. It's my night off from being spiritual. Suppose I do go. I am not saying I will, but suppose I do. What will I say?" By the way, guess who won the debate?

When Moses complained about not knowing what to say and asked God His name, the Lord spoke some of the most powerful words in the Bible. He said in Exodus 3:14, "I AM WHO I AM. This is what you are to say to the Israelites: 'I AM has sent me to you.'"

People and nations back then had a god for everything—grape god, plant god, sheep god, moon god, sun god, water god and so forth. The name of a particular god revealed his nature, purpose and character. What kind of God was the God of Israel? His name says it all—and without any limitations. The name "I AM" is translated from the Hebrew *Yahweh,* or more commonly *Jehovah.*

Because the name is all-inclusive, throughout the Bible God keeps giving us glimpses of the different parts of His nature. *Jehovah, I AM,* is combined with one facet of His nature, often in relationship to how He has just revealed Himself in response to human need. When there is lack, He is *Jehovah Jireh*—"I am your Provider." When there is stress, turmoil or war, He is

Jehovah Shalom—"I am your Peace." When sickness, disease and injury strike, He is *Jehovah Rapha*—"I am your healer." When loss and defeat seem certain, He is *Jehovah Nissi*—"the Lord your banner of victory." When we are all alone and lonely, He is *Jehovah Shammah*—"the God who is there." There are many more, for whatever the need, one aspect of His character is ever present to meet that need. He is the great I AM.

"I AM" is the covenant name for God. It is such a sacred and magnificent name that to this day Orthodox Jews will not pronounce the name when they read the Scriptures. In fact, the word *Jehovah* evolved from the more correct *Yahweh* for that very reason. The vowels from *Adonai,* one of the Hebrew terms for Lord, were inserted between the consonants of *Yahweh* to remind the Jewish readers not to say the sacred name. The consonants of *Yahweh* with the vowels of *Adonai* eventually became our word *Jehovah*.

The name is not only sacred, but it is also powerful. In John 18:3–6, Jesus perhaps gave us a glimpse into His divine nature when His accusers came to arrest Him. He asked the Roman guards, "Who are you looking for?"

"We are looking for Jesus of Nazareth," they replied.

Jesus said, "I am He."

While this is not a mistranslation, in the Greek Jesus literally proclaimed, "I am." I think, judging by the reaction of the people, He was not merely identifying Himself as the one they were looking for, but giving them all a peek into His true divine nature.

> When Jesus said, "I am he," they drew back and fell to
> the ground.
>
> —JOHN 18:6

Talk about the power of God and being slain in the Spirit! His enemies did not stand a chance.

Not knowing what to say or what to do when called into the service of God is no excuse. *I AM* has sent you, and *I AM* will provide you with whatever you need in word or deed.

"WHAT IF THEY DON'T BELIEVE ME?"

Moses still wasn't convinced. Now he was concerned not just with himself, but with the response he would get.

> What if they do not believe me or listen to me and say, "The LORD did not appear to you?"
> —EXODUS 4:1

When called into ministry it is not our job to worry about results. I cannot save, heal or deliver anybody. Only God can do that. I can do my part, but the results are in the hands of the Lord. In the case of Moses, God allowed him to glimpse the signs and wonders He would perform, which would give Moses credibility with the people and with Pharaoh. Likewise, if we embark on a work that is truly of God, we will see signs and wonders on our behalf that will convince our critics that our work is the Lord's.

"I HAVE A LIMITATION"

Even then Moses was not satisfied.

> O Lord, I have never been eloquent, neither in the past nor since you have spoken to your servant. I am slow of speech and tongue.
> —EXODUS 4:10

Moses did not see himself as a gifted communicator, and a job of this magnitude certainly required personal charisma. Maybe he remembered his days in Egypt as one of the elite. He had never been the quick-witted one at parties, and in class at school he had always had trouble getting the words out even when he knew the answer.

Some think he had the kind of stuttering problem where he would get caught on words. Moses may have said to the Lord, "I-I-I-I c-c-can't. Y-y-you gotta be k-k-kidding me." If so, I can relate, for I grew up with stuttering problems, and to this day I still have those tendencies. I can control the stuttering if I stop and slow down, but it remains an ongoing challenge.

As a kid growing up in an anti-Pentecostal church, I was critical of the late Kathryn Kuhlman. To me she came across syrupy-sweet and melodramatic as she would talk very slowly and enunciate every single syllable. Years later I found out that one of the reasons she talked like that was because she too had to battle a severe stuttering problem. She had learned to talk slowly not for mere dramatic effect, but to control her stuttering. Not only did I have to repent for my childish appraisal of her ministry, but I wept as I admired her courage for not allowing her limitation to hold her back.

I clearly remember telling the Lord when He called me to preach that I would gladly do any ministry that did not involve speaking, but just as with Moses, He did not let me off the hook. Now, like Paul, I have learned to say, "When I am weak, then I am strong" (2 Cor. 12:10).

Sometimes God lets us keep a limp, a stutter or a thorn in the flesh as a reminder of what we have been delivered from and to whom the glory belongs. Limitations are not excuses; they are credentials in the hands of the great *I AM*.

"CAN'T SOMEONE ELSE DO IT?"

You would think Moses would have surrendered by now, but he wasn't done yet. As a final plea he says:

O Lord, please send someone else to do it.

—Exodus 4:13

Despite all the answers, all the assurances and all the promises, Moses still did not think he was the man for the job. Surely there were others who were better qualified and available for service. This, however, would be Moses' last stand, for the next verse says, "The LORD's anger burned against Moses." Again, guess who won the debate?

Every excuse Moses brought before the Lord was based on good reasons. He was a nobody; he didn't know what to say; the people probably wouldn't believe him; he stuttered and was not a gifted orator; somebody else probably could have done a better job. All true. But just because excuses have good reasons do not mean they are good excuses.

I had a dream when I was twenty years old that I will never forget. In this dream I was standing in line to go to heaven. I normally hate lines, but this one was fun. Everyone I saw in line was happy. We were giving each other high fives because this was the line to go to heaven. It was worth the wait.

Then I noticed right next to the line, only about ten feet away, was another long line. That was the line to go to hell. As happy as we were in our line for heaven, that's how sad those people were in their line for hell. I scanned the line, and standing directly across from me were my two best friends from high school. I felt bad for them and hoped they wouldn't see me, but they did.

"Why didn't you tell us?" they asked.

It was a good question. In high school I had been a Christian and had gone to church, but I was shy and didn't want to be pushy about my personal faith. I didn't know what to say or how to say it, and if they had asked me questions, I just knew I would have never known the answers. Besides, I was a "cool" athlete, and most of my friends thought Christians were geeks. I didn't want them to think I was a geek. If I had tried to tell them about Jesus or even invited them to church, they probably would have thought I was being too religious. They might have even rejected me.

I had all these reasons why I hadn't told them yet. And they were good reasons—all of them true. But looking directly into the eyes of my friends who were in line to go to hell, I knew all my good reasons added up to pitiful excuses.

I tried to explain to them the reasons why I had never shared the Good News with them, but they all felt like sawdust in the mouth. When I was all done, they looked at me with eyes of desperation and softly said, "Well, at least you could have tried."

I woke up in a sweat. Within two weeks I had tracked down one of my two former buddies and clearly told him about my faith in Jesus. I brought him to our college ministry at church where he accepted the Lord. My other friend I could not find. I never heard what happened to him. I still don't know. All I know is that my good reasons made bad excuses.

What are your good reasons that don't make good excuses?

"I'm Too Young"

Some of us try to tell God that we are too young. Jeremiah tried that one.

> "Ah, Sovereign LORD," I said, "I do not know how to speak; I am only a child."
>
> —JEREMIAH 1:6

Maybe you are young or feel like a baby Christian, and therefore you think the time has not yet come for God to use you. But if God calls, don't delay. He will be with you, teaching you what to say and showing you what to do. No one is too young for God.

"IT'S TOO LATE FOR ME"

Some people are convinced that life has passed them by. Their opportunities to serve the Lord in any significant way are long gone. I have had people tell me, "Pastor, I wish I would have heard that sermon forty years ago."

"Why?" I respond. "You're not dead yet. God must still have something for you, or you would be in heaven by now."

"I wish I would have obeyed the Lord years ago," others mutter.

"Why not obey now?" I reply. "Sure, it would have been better to obey twenty years ago, but now is the perfect time to get things right."

Years ago I heard Billy Graham address a group of Bible college students who were chomping at the bit to be done with their studies and get to some "real ministry." He said, "If I had only three years left to live, I would spend two of them in preparation for ministry and only one in actual ministry." He said this to encourage young people to stick with their studies. I say it to you to let you know that your entire life may only have been preparation for what God is going to do with the rest of your life. He can do so much in a brief timespan if you give Him the chance.

Jesus spent thirty years in preparation and only three in ministry. Moses was eighty before God called him to lead His people out of bondage in Egypt. It is never too late to be used by God.

"I DON'T HAVE THE SKILLS"

The prophet Amos tried that one.

> I was neither a prophet nor a prophet's son, but I was a shepherd, and I also took care of sycamore-fig trees.
> —AMOS 7:14

Amos was saying he was just an ordinary guy. He had never been to school to study under the prophets. You too might say, "I haven't been to Bible college. I haven't been to seminary. I haven't even been going to church for very long." Another good reason, but if God has called you, it is a poor excuse.

Amos's attitude was, "I'm not a prophet or a prophet's son, but I'll prophesy until a prophet comes." I like that! There are times when availability is more important to God than ability.

Amos was also from Judah, the southern kingdom, but God told him to go prophesy to Israel, the northern kingdom. That is the equivalent of God calling a southern good ole boy to minister in New York City, or a black man from Chicago to evangelize an all-white region in Georgia. We may think we are the wrong color, the wrong sex and the wrong age ministering in the wrong area. Not if God has called you.

"I'M TOO SINFUL"

This is one of the most common and destructive excuses I hear. People tell me, "If you knew about my life, you would know why I am not very quick to get involved in what God is doing."

I respond, "If you knew the God who is calling you, you would feel differently."

The prophet Isaiah tried that excuse. God needed someone to send, and Isaiah saw the Lord in a vision. Upon beholding the Lord's holiness and perfection, he cried:

> Woe to me!...I am ruined! For I am a man of unclean lips, and I live among a people of unclean lips.
> —ISAIAH 6:5

Any one of us could say that. If it is not our lips, then it is our unclean eyes, or our unclean ears, or our unclean hands, or our unclean feet, or our unclean heart. Of all the reasons not to respond to the call of God, this may be best. Who among us is clean or worthy in the presence of a righteous and holy God? Still, God will not take no for an answer.

God sent a seraph down to touch Isaiah's lips with a hot, glowing coal from the altar.

> See, this has touched your lips; your guilt is taken away
> and your sin atoned for.
>
> —ISAIAH 6:7

Yes, God can use sinful people. But He does not want to leave us in our sin any more than He wants to leave us in the valleys or in the pain of our past. He did not simply say to Isaiah, "No big deal, I'll use you in your sin." No, he delivered Isaiah from his sin. If you do not serve a God who is delivering you from sin, then you are not serving the right God.

When Jesus' birth was foretold to Joseph and Mary, the angel said:

> You are to give him the name Jesus, because he will save
> his people from their sins.
>
> —MATTHEW 1:21

Most believers today are interested in being saved from the penalty of sin. Simply put, we don't want to go to hell, and we don't want to suffer the consequences of our actions. We are pleased to receive salvation as long as we think we are escaping sin's consequences. Jesus did not come, however, to simply save us from hell. He came to save us from sin—not only sin's penalty, but also sin's power.

Drug addicts do not need to be delivered from the effects of their abuse; they need to be delivered from the power those drugs have over them. Only then can they hear the call of

God like Isaiah. Sin is no excuse, but neither does God excuse our sin.

Scott chose the wrong path as a young man and paid for it dearly. He grew up with an alcoholic father, and following his dad's lead, he began to drink at an early age, plunging headfirst into a life of unbridled sex, drugs and fighting.

One night, drunk and drugged out, he was on his way home from a beach party when he found yet another opportunity to fight. As the two men were circling each other, Scott lost his balance, fell back and hit his neck. The incident left him paralyzed.

His parents, now Christians, met him in the emergency room and shared the gospel with him. Two days later, Scott accepted the Lord and began heading in a new direction. He moved back home, earned a college degree and went to graduate school. Today he works as a marriage and family psychotherapist helping people to rebuild their lives.

Scott was not simply delivered from the penalty of sin—escaping its consequences—but he was delivered from the power of alcohol, drugs, illicit sex and violence. Breaking free from his bondages is what allowed him to rebuild his life in a way that would bless him and touch others.

God will forgive you, cleanse you, change you and use you. There are plenty of good reasons not to serve the Lord, but there are no good excuses.

Isaiah was too sinful. Jeremiah was too young. Amos was untrained and from the wrong side of the tracks. Peter was an uneducated fisherman. Paul was an overeducated scholar who hated Christians. And the list goes on. In every case, God had an answer for their shortcomings. And He will take no excuse from us either—not even the hurts of our past. God will never waste a hurt.

Notes

Chapter 1: God of the Valleys

1. Source obtained from the Internet: Franklin Delano Roosevelt's First Inaugural Address, March 4, 1933, www.re-quest.net/history/inaugurals/fdr.

Chapter 2: Valleys of Our Own Mistakes

1. Source obtained from the Internet: John Singleton, "John Wesley's marriage reveals his humanity," www.umr.org/Dec30/marriage.
2. Source obtained from the Internet: Chuck Shepherd's News of the Weird, www.newsoftheweird.com.
3. Ibid.
4. Ibid.
5. Ibid.
6. Source obtained from the Internet: "Slightly OffCenter," *USA Today Update,* June 22, 2000, www.usatoday.com.
7. No information available.
8. "Amazing Grace" by John Newton. Public domain.

Chapter 3: Valleys Others Put Us Through

1. Kimberly Hefling, "Hatfields and McCoys play softball game," Associated Press, June 11, 2000.

Chapter 4: Valleys of Sovereignty

1. Associated Press, *San Francisco Chronicle,* June 15, 2000, A4.
2. Edward John Carnell, *An Introduction to Christian Apologetics* (Grand Rapids, MI: Eerdmans, 1948), 277.
3. Bertrand Russell, *Why I Am Not a Christian* (London: Allen and Unwin, 1957). 157.

Chapter 5: Giants in the Valley

1. C. S. Lewis, *The Problem of Pain* (New York: Macmillan Co., 1944), 81.

Chapter 8: Miracles Can Happen As Suddenly As Tragedies

1. Source obtained from the Internet: Career Highlights, Kurt Warner (13), sports.nfl.com/2000/playerhighlights?id=2477; "Storybook ending," sportsillustrated.cnn.com/football/nfl/2000/playoffs.
2. "Bills 1964 Championship Ring Found," Associated Press, July 14, 2000.

Chapter 11: How to Turn a Little Into a Lot

1. Source obtained from the Internet: Chuck Shepherd's News of the Weird, www.newsoftheweird.com.

You can experience more of God's grace & love!

If you would like free information on how you can know God more deeply and experience His grace, love and power more fully in your life, simply write or e-mail us. We'll be delighted to send you information that will be a blessing to you.

To check out other titles from **Creation House** that will impact your life, be sure to visit your local Christian bookstore, or call this toll-free number:

1-800-599-5750

For free information from Creation House:

CREATION HOUSE
600 Rinehart Rd.
Lake Mary, FL 32746
www.creationhouse.com